Ame

Impressionism

By H. Barbara Weinberg

RIZZOLI ART SERIES

Series Editor: Norma Broude

American Impressionism

American Impressionism developed in the 1880s in response to American painters' appreciation of the works of the French Impressionists, who, in the late 1860s, had renounced academic standards of subject choice and style in favor of highly chromatic, rapidly rendered portrayals of ordinary experience. The leading avant-garde movement in painting in the United States until about 1900, American Impressionism was then challenged by Robert Henri and the Ashcan School, a group of artists who wished to portray modern life more candidly—especially its grittier aspects—and by American practitioners of Cubism, Fauvism, and other modernist movements that were introduced to a broad public at the 1913 Armory Show in New York. These challenges notwithstanding, some of the leading American Impressionists continued to paint works of interest and quality until about the time of World War I. Thereafter, American Impressionism increasingly lost the esteem of collectors and scholars as they turned away from art that was so clearly based on European styles and that recalled the gentility of the Gilded Age.

Beginning in the 1960s, the extraordinary growth in the market value of French Impressionist paintings rekindled interest in American Impressionism, which was more accessible and more affordable. Concurrently, scholars and writers came to accept that what was American in late nineteenth-century American art was its cosmopolitan spirit and therefore began to reexamine American Impressionism. Numerous recent exhibitions, books, and articles and the attention of new and veteran collectors to American Impressionist paintings suggest that enthusiasm for them is at a peak. We find pleasure and, perhaps, solace in the American Impressionists' vivid record of a lively and fascinating—yet simpler and gentler—period, in their celebrations of familiar sites abroad and at home, in their portrayals of genteel people and sunny places.

American Impressionism developed toward the end of a period in which American painting in general had been transformed by a desire to emulate foreign—especially French—models.[1] In the decades just after the Civil War, American collectors had filled their walls with contemporary French academic and Barbizon School paintings.[2] In order to compete for patronage with their foreign rivals, unprecedented numbers of American painters went abroad, usually to Paris. There they assimilated the academic style—subjects invented from historical and literary texts, developed from extensive study of the nude human figure, and executed with technical finesse and high finish—or the Barbizon School's love for poetic landscape, studied outdoors but rendered in the studio.[3]

The internationalism of American art in the 1870s and 1880s derived not only from the fact that French standards were highly esteemed, but from the general temper of the period in the United States The nation was experiencing profound conflict between the country's fading rural tradition and the emerging industrialism and urbanism. Active memories of the divisive Civil War, brutal labor strikes, pressures of immigration, and political unrest challenged national identity and pride and invited a certain escapism. The United States began to participate more than ever before in worldwide economic, political, and social affairs, and this, too, abetted internationalism in taste and art.

The American painters who would turn to Impressionism were exemplars of internationalism. They learned their early lessons in American academies that had been formed, or reformed, according to the standards of the Ecole des Beaux-Arts—the official French government school—with teachers who had studied in Paris just after the Civil War. They then went to Paris for additional study of Beaux-Arts principles—either at the Ecole itself or at such new schools as the Académie Julian that had similar curricula—they spent time in the galleries of the Louvre or Luxembourg, and they even worked in artists' colonies such as Barbizon.

For example, a variety of French stylistic influences and internationalist subject interests affected the early works of Theodore Robinson. He had studied at the National Academy of Design, New York, in the mid-1870s and was a founder of New York's Art Students League, which also taught Beaux-Arts principles. From 1875 to 1879 and from 1884 to 1887, Robinson worked in Paris under several fairly conservative teachers, including Jean-Léon Gérôme, the most popular Beaux-Arts master among American students, and Carolus-Duran, an antiacademic portraitist. Their approaches ranged from the devoutly academic to the more liberal. Robinson voiced the prevailing American quest for internationalism in a letter to a painter friend in May 1883. Describing his subject interests, he noted: "I have nearly got rid of the desire to do 'American things'—mostly because American life is so unpaintable—and a higher kind of art seems to me to exclude the questions of nationality."[4]

The French painters who would be called Impressionists had made their debut in a group exhibition in April 1874; they would show together until 1886, eight times in all. Their commitment to portraying the contemporary local scene and their lively technique and interest in brilliant outdoor light challenged the academic standards that American art students had learned at home and reinforced abroad. Generally, the new movement in painting attracted little notice from aspiring American painters in Paris, including the future American Impressionists, most of whom were there in its heyday. The French Impressionists' exhibitions on the grand boulevards near the Opera House were distant from the Latin Quarter and Montmartre academies. And since many of the Americans had scraped together precious funds for limited Parisian study, they would have followed their teachers' advice to visit the museums and not waste time at dissident exhibitions. Academic acolytes, they would have scorned the Impressionists' paintings, if they saw them at all.

Exceptions to the rule, two American painters, Mary Cassatt and John Singer Sargent, caught the spirit of the new movement in French painting in the mid to late 1870s and

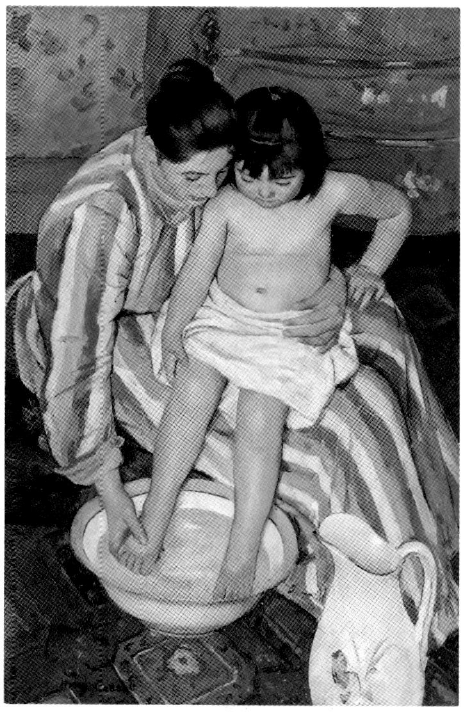

1. Mary Cassatt. *The Bath.* 1891–1892. Oil on canvas, 39½ × 26". © 1989 The Art Institute of Chicago. Robert A. Waller Fund, 1910.2

were bold enough to join in Impressionist experiments. Cassatt had studied first in Philadelphia and had then followed a peripatetic course of European training and travel before she settled permanently in Paris in 1874. A portrait that she showed in the 1874 Salon drew favorable notice from Edgar Degas, who in 1877 invited her to show with the Impressionists. Cassatt exhibited with them four times between 1879 and 1886. Most of her paintings such as *At the Opera* (plate 1) and *The Bath* (fig. 1), whether or not they were shown with those of the Impressionists, reveal strong sympathies with their efforts—including a devotion to straightforward accounts of everyday experience, bold composition, and spirited brushwork. Cassatt also brought to her paintings the viewpoint of an empathetic but unsentimental witness to the lives of women at a time when traditional gender roles, like much else in contemporary life, were being transformed.

By 1879 Sargent had completed his studies with Carolus-Duran and was building a reputation as a painter of stylish portraits. He had also begun his lifelong habit of painting subject pictures of the sort that the Impressionists preferred, departing from his usual activity as a portraitist to work out of doors. Such informal works always refreshed Sargent's activity as a portraitist; they kept him in touch with the actualities of appearance of people, places, and atmosphere outside the studio and helped him seize the suggestion of a specific moment. Sargent's subject pictures would be enhanced in turn by his gift for characterization, often including astute and individualized records of his models. Sargent's 1879 canvas *In the Luxembourg Gardens* (plate 2) declared his sympathy with the new movement in French painting. As the French Impressionists often did, Sargent recorded a vignette of modern Paris, which had been transformed by Emperor Napoleon III with public parks such as the Luxembourg Gardens in response to urban overcrowding.[5] For his interest in commonplace urban incident, as well as for his rapid stroke and brilliant palette, Sargent took his example from Claude Monet, whom he probably met in 1876, and from Degas, Edouard Manet, Pierre-Auguste Renoir, and Gustave Caillebotte.

In such paintings as *Paul Helleu Sketching with His Wife* (plate 9), painted in Fladbury, England, after a visit to Monet at his home in Giverny in the spring of 1889, Sargent personalized the French master's chromatic palette and high key with a distinctive spiky stroke and a portrait painter's interest in specific individuals. The painting, depicting another successful portraitist and his wife, is also emblematic of the commitment made by Sargent and his Impressionist colleagues to working outdoors and directly in contact with nature.

By contrast with Cassatt and Sargent, most of the future American Impressionalists were immersed in the 1870s in academic study and were reluctant to abandon traditional principles. Typically, J. Alden Weir, then a student of Gérôme, was disdainful when he saw the third Impressionist exhibition in the spring of 1877. He wrote home: "I saw a show of a new school which call themselves 'Impressionalists.' I never in my life saw more horrible things. . . . They do not observe drawing nor form but give you an impression of what they call nature. It was worse than the Chamber of Horrors."[6] Not until French Impressionism became more familiar and was validated in the art marketplace of the later 1880s—especially by pioneering American patrons—did Americans such as Robinson and Weir decide to adopt its palette and procedures.

Manet was the first artist associated with French Impressionism to receive critical attention in the United States, beginning in the mid-1870s. In 1881 Weir, assisted by the painter William Merritt Chase, helped the New York collector Erwin Davis to acquire two of Manet's paintings; Davis gave these to the Metropolitan Museum of Art in 1887. In 1877 Louisine Elder, later Mrs. Havemeyer, with Cassatt's advice purchased a pastel by Degas and lent it to the 1878 annual exhibition of the American Water Color Society, where it was received with modest enthusiasm. In 1879 a comprehensive account of Impressionism in *Lippincott's Magazine* described the movement for American readers but criticized the apparently bizarre palette and the sketchiness of many French Impressionist paintings.[7]

Several large exhibitions increased American interest in French Impressionism in the 1880s. In 1883 the Foreign Exhibition Association brought to Boston a show assembled by the French Impressionists' foremost dealer, Paul Durand-Ruel. Canvases by Monet, Renoir, Camille Pissarro, and Alfred Sisley were exhibited. At the end of the same year, Chase guided the selection of a display of paintings at the Pedestal Fund Art Loan Exhibition in New York that included Davis's two Manets and a bold Degas ballet scene.[8] In 1886 Durand-Ruel exhibited 290 works at New York's American Art Association. The paintings and pastels, including dozens by each of the leading French Impressionists, provoked extensive commentary in the press. Sales of Impressionist works from the exhibition also indicated that American collectors were ready to support the radical art. The precocious patrons—Davis, the Havemeyers, and Alexander Cassatt, the painter's brother—were joined by others whose interest would encourage American painters to explore the style.

Chase was probably the first major American artist to paint Impressionist canvases in the United States. Trained in Munich, he had been attracted to the dissident paintings of Wilhelm Leibl, the German alter ego of the French Realist

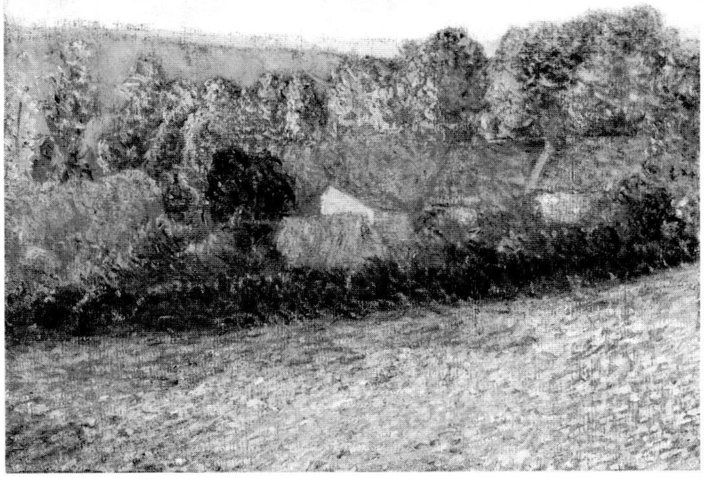

2. Lilla Cabot Perry. *Autumn Afternoon, Giverny.* n.d. Oil on canvas, 25¾ × 31¾". Courtesy of Terra Museum of American Art, Chicago. Daniel J. Terra Collection

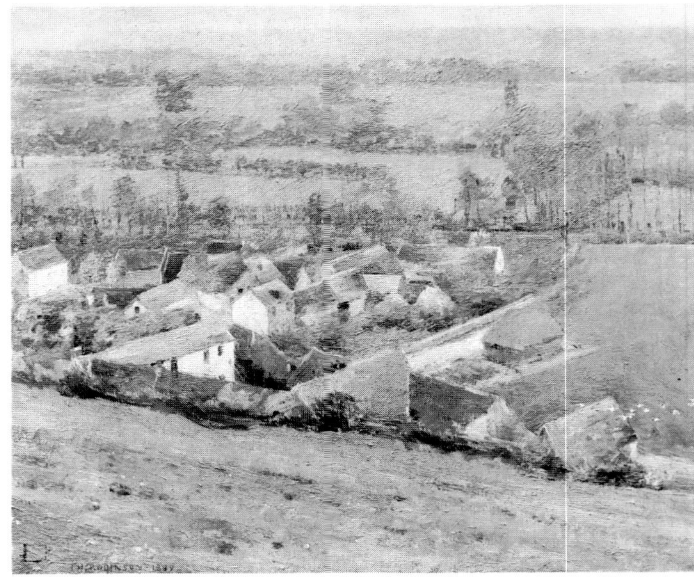

3. Theodore Robinson. *Bird's-Eye View, Giverny.* 1889. Oil on canvas, 15 1/16 × 22". The Metropolitan Museum of Art, New York

Gustave Courbet. Chase was thus detached from Beaux-Arts prejudices and more likely than his Paris-trained colleagues to become an Impressionist without a struggle. As early as 1885 Chase did this in his views of Central and Prospect parks in New York (plate 3). These freely brushed, light-filled paintings take viewers to familiar places that were created in response to urban growth and that allowed residents to establish perforce a new relationship with nature and to enjoy a reminder of rural life. Redolent objects of national and civic pride, New York's great parks were ideal analogues of those that Manet, Degas, Sargent, and others had painted in Paris. The parks also echoed the fundamental aspect of Chase's aesthetically furnished New York studio (see fig. 4), insofar as they were artistically arranged accumulations of eye-pleasing elements, and therefore must have had a particular appeal for him.

By the later 1880s there were signs of dawning awareness of French Impressionism among American painters in Paris. For example, Childe Hassam painted city scenes using the Impressionists' high-keyed palette. Perhaps because Hassam had already painted Boston sites, albeit under the influence of such conservative urban painters as Giuseppe de Nittis, he was attracted to the Impressionists' Paris views.[9] Moreover, because he sought French academic instruction only after maturing as a painter, he may have been a less malleable academic aspirant at Julian's than the other future American Impressionists had been and therefore more open to the new painting.

By 1887 several American painters—including Robinson, Willard Metcalf, Theodore Wendel, and John Leslie Breck—had been drawn to Giverny, first by the charm of the village itself, only a few hours northwest of Paris by train, and then by the presence of Monet, who had settled there in May 1883.[10] Among the Americans who would return to the United States with an especially keen understanding of Monet's accomplishments was Lilla Cabot Perry. She would spend nine summers at Giverny between 1889 and 1909, was acquainted with Monet by 1891, purchased his works and brought them back to Boston, spoke and wrote about him for American audiences, and altered her academic style according to the example of his chromatic landscapes (see fig. 2).

A dual academic-Impressionist manner is evident in Robinson's Giverny paintings (fig. 3). Reluctant to renounce his academic lessons and to allow forms to dissolve in corrosive light, he carefully articulated individual volumes before covering them with a chromatic Impressionist veneer of broken strokes.[11] Reflecting Monet's increasing interest in unmistakably French vernacular images,[12] Robinson recorded Giverny's characteristic yellow stucco walls and red tile rooftops. He thus seems to have laid the foundation for his pursuit of nationally resonant subjects after his return to the United States in 1892.

After completing their studies, some American painters remained in Europe to follow academic and Barbizon impulses or, as in the case of Cassatt and, more intermittently, of Sargent, to work as Impressionists. Others returned home, usually to New York, where in the late nineteenth century American artistic energy was consolidated. New York's interest in art is exemplified by Chase's activities: He was able to install himself in a studio building constructed specifically for the use of artists (fig. 4), he could participate in many exhibiting organizations, including the Society of American Artists—founded in 1877 to serve younger artists who had studied in Europe—and he taught at the Art Students League, one of many new venues for instruction.

As repatriated painters became aware of the growing American patronage for Impressionist works, many of them gave up traditional modes and adopted the new style, usually tempering it with a measure of academic control. Robinson, Hassam, Perry, and others who had learned Impressionism through direct contact with French mentors and their works, were important conduits of the style to their compatriots upon their return. And of course their lessons were reinforced by the French Impressionist paintings that could now be seen in American private collections and public exhibitions.

It may at first appear that the American Impressionists merely went through the motions of adopting Impressionism's surfaces, motivated by commercial concerns. They had, after all, been immersed in French styles and they may have simply moved on from the academic to the manner of the Impressionists, just as American patrons had moved on to build more up-to-date collections. However, further con-

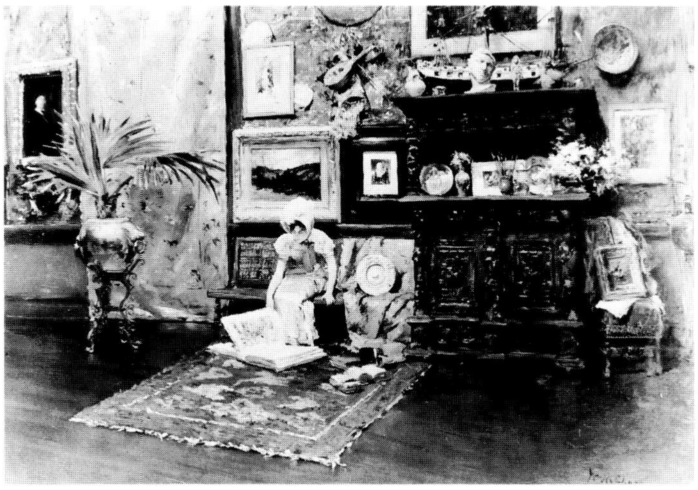

4. William Merritt Chase. *In the Studio*. c.1880. Oil on canvas, 28⅛ × 40¹⁄₁₆". The Brooklyn Museum. Gift of Mrs. Carl H. DeSilver in memory of her husband

sideration suggests that the leading American Impressionists grasped the essential spirit of their new mentors' engagement with the contemporary local scene and followed them in responding to the here and now of actual experience. Their sympathy for French Impressionism seems to have been inevitable, given their pattern of interest in French art and the material and cultural energy of the United States, which intensified the changes in modern life that had generated Impressionism in France.

American Impressionism also provided a remedy to the saturation of American art by European academic and Barbizon influence. By the end of the 1880s critics who had earlier urged American artists to abandon nationalism—to accept the idea that American life was unpaintable, as Robinson had complained in May 1883—now worried that a recognizably American art had disappeared. Possibly in response to these critics, as well as independently, the American Impressionists seem to have reversed their earlier internationalist stance. They began to seek out American subjects that were genuine counterparts—not just imitations—of French Impressionist subjects, to portray American subjects that had local or national resonance or that announced American progress. It is even possible that the American Impressionists' stylistic cautiousness, a residue of their academic training, was reinforced by their wish to be true to the subjects they depicted.

A nationalistic spirit was expressed in styles other than Impressionism in the late 1880s and 1890s—in the late works of Winslow Homer, for example,[13] and in the historical murals that academic painters provided for public buildings. Not every American Impressionist was a nationalist: Cassatt and Sargent depicted modern life in France, and later expatriates such as Richard E. Miller and Frederick Carl Frieseke painted Impressionist canvases with little American sentiment. That said, there are enough instances to suggest that the repatriated American Impressionists were not just imitating the surfaces of French Impressionism but were articulating the spirit of their own time and place in the new style.

Representing modern American life was a challenge for painters. In the late 1880s and 1890s the transformation from an agrarian to an industrialized urban society created tension between the thrill of change and nostalgia for the rural past. Some American painters who adhered to traditional styles—Thomas Eakins, for example—did portray contemporary local subjects. But having assimilated the substance of French Impressionism, it was the best of the American Impressionists who became most consistently engaged with modern life. Satisfied with the vignette rather than the grand composition, they could respond nimbly to the bustling spirit and the fragmented experience that marked the modern age.

It is obvious that the American Impressionists had conflicted feelings about modern life, were simultaneously enthusiastic about its pervasive energy and regretful that much of what was reassuring and familiar was being swept away by progress. They ignored problems of race, immigration, and urban poverty, preferring to turn a positive light on the American scene. Their tendency to enhance reality accorded with the attitudes of writers such as William Dean Howells, who recommended in *Criticism and Fiction* (1891) that writers should "concern themselves with the more smiling aspects of life, which are the more American."[14] Since political, economic, and social confusion would not substantially subside until the administration of President Theodore Roosevelt in the early twentieth century, euphemistic views of the American scene in an Impressionist style are not surprising.

The American Impressionists' personal backgrounds would also have conditioned their emphasis on refinement and even their genteel resistance to the most threatening aspects of modern America. Like Cassatt, the daughter of an affluent Pennsylvania family, and Sargent, whose ancestors included merchants in colonial Gloucester, Massachusetts, most of the repatriated American Impressionists came from comfortable Anglo-Saxon families long established in the United States. New England connections were very strong: Frank W. Benson and Hassam were sons of wealthy Massachusetts merchants; the families of Robinson, Edmund Tarbell, and Dennis Miller Bunker were less prosperous but no less established; Perry was descended from Boston's Cabots and Lowells; and Edward Emerson Simmons, a relative of Ralph Waldo Emerson, grew up in the Old Manse in Concord, Massachusetts. The socioeconomic profile of the group is blurred only slightly by the fact that Metcalf was the son of a loom tender and carpenter from Lowell, Massachusetts; that John Henry Twachtman was the son of German immigrants of modest circumstances; and that Chase acquired rather than inherited his connections to the upper middle class in New York City and Long Island's Southampton.

A few instances may suffice to suggest the pattern of American Impressionists' choosing subjects that emanate from and aggrandize their experience of America at the turn of the last century. Echoing Chase's portrayal of New York's celebrated public parks, Simmons painted *Boston Public Garden* in 1893 (plate 5). This twenty-four-acre park connects old Boston—Beacon Hill, where the statehouse dome looms, and the Common—to new Boston, forming the front yard of the newly developed Back Bay. Softening it with a covering of snow, Simmons emphasizes the Public Garden's rural quality and its ability to bring nature into the heart of the city. Hassam's *Charles River and Beacon Hill* (plate 4) also contains a meditation on the contrast between old and new, juxtaposing the distant statehouse with the "water side of Beacon," where Howells's nouveau-riche Silas Lapham built his ill-fated Back Bay dream house.[15]

The American Impressionists turned away from or sani-

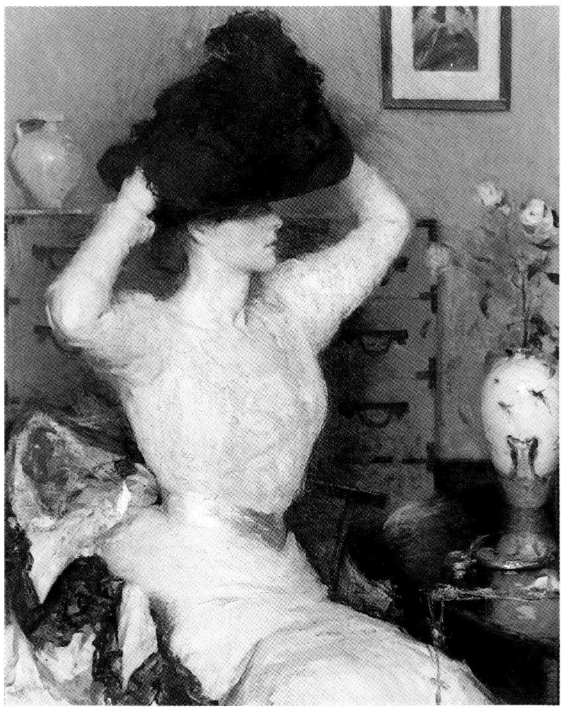

5. Frank W. Benson. *The Black Hat*. 1904. Oil on canvas, 40 × 32". Museum of Art, Rhode Island School of Design, Providence, Rhode Island. Gift of Walter Callender, Henry D. Sharpe, Howard L. Clark, William Gammell, and Isaac C. Bates

tized the unpleasant facts of industrialization. In *The Red Bridge* (plate 8), for example, Weir treated a modern New England railroad bridge as an elegant chromatic note embedded in harmonious nature and conducting a dialogue with graceful tree limbs. They portrayed ladies at leisure, relaxing on a brilliant afternoon in the artist's garden, as in Tarbell's *Three Sisters: A Study in June Sunlight* (plate 6), at a coastal resort, as in Chase's *At the Seaside* (plate 13), or trying on a stylish hat in the privacy of an elegant home, as in Benson's *The Black Hat* (fig. 5). They also recalled a simpler American past, recording, as Robinson did in 1893, a disused Catskills canal (plate 7) that had been rendered obsolete by the railroad.

Many of the American Impressionists found inspiration in New England scenery, answering urbanization and industrialization with reminders of colonial settlement and rural quietude. Bunker, inspired by Sargent's example, adopted an Impressionist palette and bold composition in 1889 to depict *The Pool, Medfield* (plate 10), a scene in a New England village that had been part of the Massachusetts Bay Colony. Breck came inland from the Boston estuary of the Charles River, ignoring urban developments to record a decorative vignette in *Grey Day on the Charles* (plate 12), an American analogue of Monet's portrayals of the Seine at Giverny. Throughout the 1890s Twachtman was inspired by Connecticut's frozen brooks to produce poetic canvases such as *Winter Harmony* (plate 11). And Metcalf found an American Giverny at Gloucester, a town that possessed both strong associations with the American past and extraordinary light that could nourish an Impressionist's out-of-doors work (plate 14).

Hassam's *Allies Day, May 1917* (plate 15), one of some thirty flag images that he painted between 1916 and 1919, sums up key traits of American Impressionism, including its durability into the early twentieth century despite the dual challenges of Ashcan School realism and burgeoning modernism. The view is of New York's Fifth Avenue from the northeast corner of 52nd Street, looking northward as morning sunlight strikes the facades on the west side of the avenue. Hassam's canvas was painted in response to the patriotic parades that were staged in May 1917, just after the United States entered World War I.[16] Groupings of the flags of the three allies—Great Britain, France, and the United States—appear in several places, the harmony among the three nations coincidentally stated by the fact that their three banners are variations on the theme of red, white, and blue. But ascendant at the center of the composition, the American flag is the only major banner that is not interrupted by a flagpole or partially obscured by another flag. An intentional counterpart of Monet's flag-filled streetscapes, Hassam's *Allies Day, May 1917* is also characteristic of American Impressionism in its optimistic celebration of the modern metropolis and modern America and in its nationalistic sentiment.

NOTES

1. Some of the ideas explored in this essay were discussed with Doreen Bolger, Curator, Amon Carter Museum, Fort Worth, Texas, and David Park Curry, Curator of American Arts, Virginia Museum of Fine Arts, Richmond, in the course of our jointly preparing the catalogue for the exhibition *American Impressionism and Realism: The Painting of Modern Life, 1885–1915* (New York: The Metropolitan Museum of Art, forthcoming).
2. The best account of the phenomenon appears in Edward Strahan [Earl Shinn], *The Art Treasures of America*, 3 vols. (Philadelphia: George Barrie, 1879–[1882]; reprint, New York: Garland, 1977).
3. For the American pursuit of foreign training, see Michael Quick, *American Expatriate Painters of the Late Nineteenth Century* (Dayton, Ohio: Dayton Art Institute, 1976); Lois Marie Fink, *American Art at the Nineteenth-Century Paris Salons* (New York: Cambridge University Press, 1990); H. Barbara Weinberg, *The Lure of Paris: Nineteenth-Century American Painters and Their French Teachers* (New York: Abbeville Press, 1991). For American emulation of Barbizon art, see Peter Bermingham, *American Art in the Barbizon Mood* (Washington, D.C.: National Collection of Fine Arts, Smithsonian Institution, 1975).
4. Theodore Robinson to Kenyon Cox, New York, May 31, 1883, Kenyon Cox Papers, Avery Architectural and Fine Arts Library, Columbia University.
5. For the significance of Paris to the French Impressionists, see Theodore Reff, *Manet and Modern Paris* (Washington, D.C.: National Gallery of Art, 1982); T[imothy]. J. Clark, *The Painting of Modern Life: Paris in the Art of Manet and His Followers* (Princeton, N.J.: Princeton University Press, 1984); Robert L. Herbert, *Impressionism: Art, Leisure, and Parisian Society* (New Haven and London: Yale University Press, 1988).
6. J. Alden Weir to his parents, Paris, April 15, 1877; quoted in Dorothy Weir Young, *The Life and Letters of J. Alden Weir* (New Haven, Conn.: Yale University Press, 1960; reprint, New York: Kennedy Graphics and Da Capo, 1971), p. 123.
7. L. Lejeune, "The Impressionist School of Painting," *Lippincott's Magazine*, vol. 24 (December 1879), pp. 720–727.
8. For a detailed discussion of this exhibition and the European paintings included in it, see Maureen C. O'Brien et al., *In Support of Liberty: European Paintings at the 1883 Pedestal Fund Art Loan Exhibition* (Southampton, N.Y.: Parrish Art Museum, 1986).
9. See Jennifer A. Martin Bienenstock, "Childe Hassam's Early Boston Cityscapes," *Arts Magazine*, vol. 55 (November 1980), pp. 168–171.
10. For discussion of the American painters at Giverny, see William H. Gerdts, *Monet's Giverny: An Impressionist Colony* (New York: Abbeville Press, 1993).
11. I first posited that the cautiousness of American Impressionism was rooted in its academic armature in "Robert Reid: Academic Impressionist," *Archives of American Art Journal*, vol. 15, no. 1 (1975), pp. 2–11, and developed the idea in "American Impressionism in Cosmopolitan Context," *Arts Magazine*, vol. 55 (November 1980), pp. 160–165.
12. See Paul Hayes Tucker, *Monet in the '90s: The Series Paintings* (Boston: Museum of Fine Arts, in association with Yale University Press, 1989).
13. Bruce Robertson, *Reckoning with Winslow Homer: His Late Paintings and Their Influence* (Cleveland: Cleveland Museum of Art in cooperation with Indiana University Press, 1990).
14. W[illiam]. D[ean]. Howells, *Criticism and Fiction* (New York: Harper and Brothers, 1891), p. 128.
15. William Dean Howells, *The Rise of Silas Lapham* (1885; New York: Viking Penguin, 1986), p. 32.
16. Ilene Susan Fort, *The Flag Paintings of Childe Hassam* (Los Angeles: Los Angeles County Museum of Art, 1988), p. 46.

FURTHER READING

Boyle, Richard J. *American Impressionism*. Boston: New York Graphic Society, 1974.

Gerdts, William H. *American Impressionism*. New York: Abbeville Press, 1984. Contains an extensive bibliography.

———. *American Impressionism: Masterworks from Public and Private Collections*, exh. cat. Lugano-Castagnola, Switzerland: Thyssen-Bornemisza Foundation, 1990.

———. *Monet's Giverny: An Impressionist Colony*. New York: Abbeville Press, 1993.

Hiesinger, Ulrich W. *Impressionism in America: The Ten American Painters*. Munich: Prestel-Verlag, 1991.

Hoopes, Donelson F. *The American Impressionists*. New York: Watson-Guptill Publications, 1972.

Lasting Impressions: American Painters in France, 1865–1915, exh. cat., essay by William H. Gerdts. Giverny, France: Musée Américain, 1992.

Ten American Painters, exh. cat., essays by William H. Gerdts et al. New York: Spanierman Gallery, 1990.

Weinberg, H. Barbara, Doreen Bolger, and David Park Curry. *American Impressionism and Realism: The Painting of Modern Life, 1885–1915*, exh. cat. New York: The Metropolitan Museum of Art, forthcoming.

First published in 1994 in the United States of America by
Rizzoli International Publications, Inc.
300 Park Avenue South
New York, New York 10010

Library of Congress Cataloging-in-Publication Data
Weinberg, H. Barbara (Helene Barbara), 1942–
American impressionism / by H. Barbara Weinberg
p. cm. — (Rizzoli art series)
Includes bibliographical references.
ISBN 0-8478-1790-3
1. Impressionism (Art)—United States. 2. Painting, American. 3. Painting, Modern—19th century—United States. 4. Painting, Modern—20th century—United States. I. Title. II. Series.
ND210.5.I4W45 1994
759. 13'09'034—dc20 93-43142
CIP

Series Editor: Norma Broude
Series designed by José Conde/Bessas & Ackerman
Editor: Charles Miers; Assistant Editor: Cathryn Drake;
Photo research: Amelia Costigan; Compositor: Rose Scarpetis

Printed in Italy

Front cover: see colorplate 1

Index to Colorplates

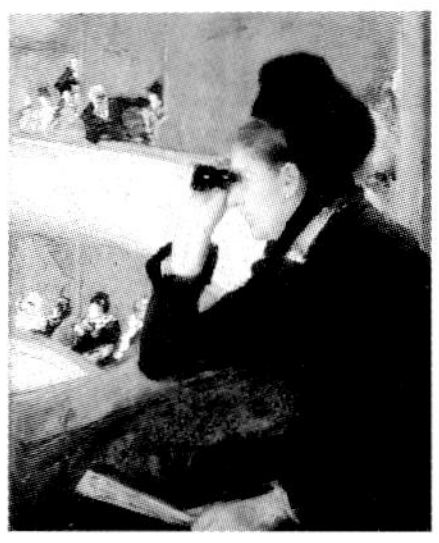

1. Mary Cassatt. *At the Opera.* 1879. An elegantly dressed woman surveys others in the audience for the matinee, indifferent to the scrutiny of the man in a distant box. While the broadly brushed planes of dramatic black pigment and the candid composition suggest Cassatt's susceptibility to Manet's influence, her portrayal of a woman engaged with her world reflects her own experience.

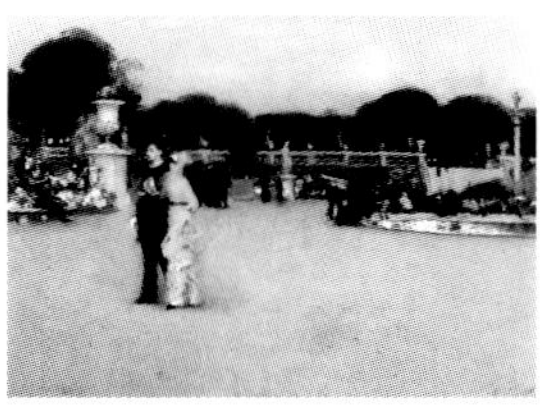

2. John Singer Sargent. *In the Luxembourg Gardens.* 1879. The Luxembourg Gardens, a popular Left Bank park, was in the news in 1879 when its administration was turned over to the Senate of France. Sargent joined the French Impressionists in portraying such a familiar place filled with ordinary citizens enjoying the pleasures of the modern city.

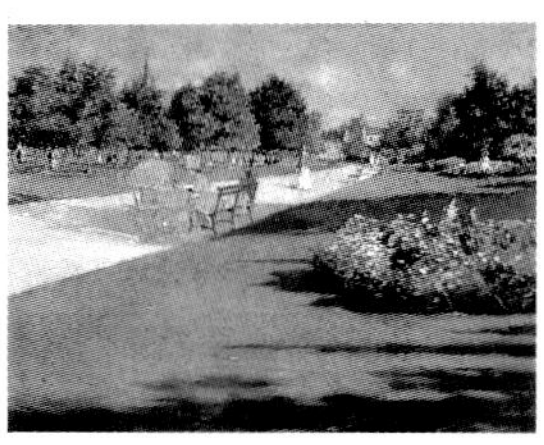

3. William Merritt Chase. *Prospect Park, Brooklyn.* c.1886. Chase created the first Impressionist paintings in the United States in New York's recently completed Central Park and Prospect Park, celebrating them as genteel, pastoral retreats from the bustle of the growing city. He seizes nature both entirely controlled and a bit wild with a freedom and freshness stimulated by his experiments in pastel.

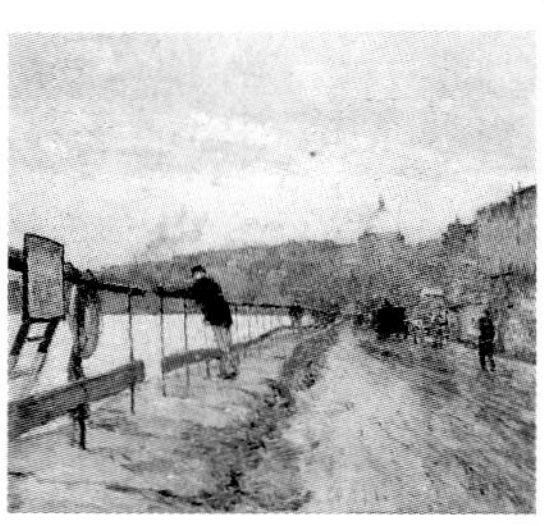

4. Frederick Childe Hassam. *Charles River and Beacon Hill.* c.1892. Hassam found ample material for city scenes in New York and in Boston. In *Charles River and Beacon Hill* he suggests a dialogue between the newly developed Back Bay—its Beacon Street backyards lining the still-unpaved promenade along the Charles River—and old Boston with its gilded Massachusetts statehouse dome in the distance.

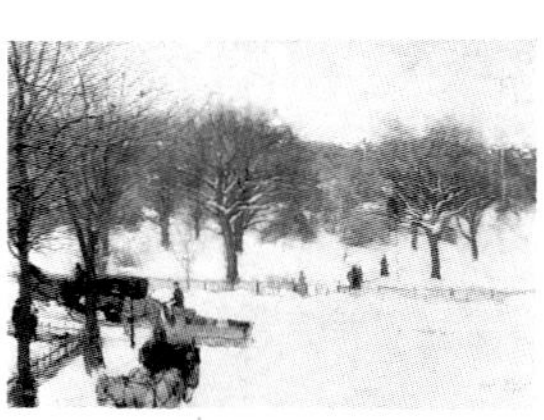

5. Edward Emerson Simmons. *Boston Public Garden.* 1893. After study in Boston and in Paris, Simmons settled in New York in 1893. Active as a muralist in the 1890s, he occasionally painted such fine Impressionist canvases as this one. Connecting Beacon Hill and the Common to the new Back Bay, the Public Garden offered Bostonians a reminder of rural quietude and respite from busy streets.

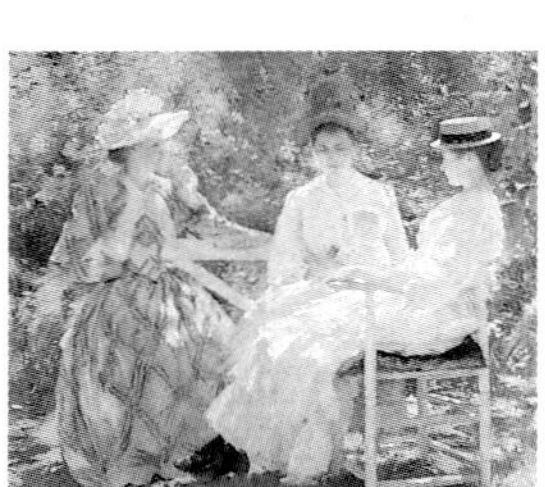

6. Edmund Tarbell. *Three Sisters: A Study in June Sunlight.* 1890. Three ladies at leisure include the painter's wife wearing a red hat and holding her daughter on her lap. Mrs. Tarbell's stylishly dressed sisters bracket her. The leader of the Boston School of painters, Tarbell created genteel New England counterparts to the French Impressionists' informal group portraits of women.

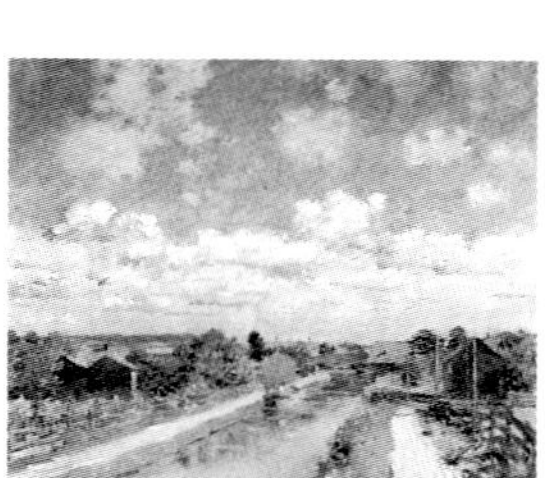

7. Theodore Robinson. *Port Ben, Delaware and Hudson Canal.* 1893. Subject to Catskills winter weather, the 108-mile-long Delaware and Hudson Canal was challenged by parallel railroads and abandoned in 1904. The quietude of disuse pervades Robinson's scene. Having worked in Monet's company at Giverny from 1888 until his return home in 1892, Robinson was especially interested in the nuances of outdoor light.

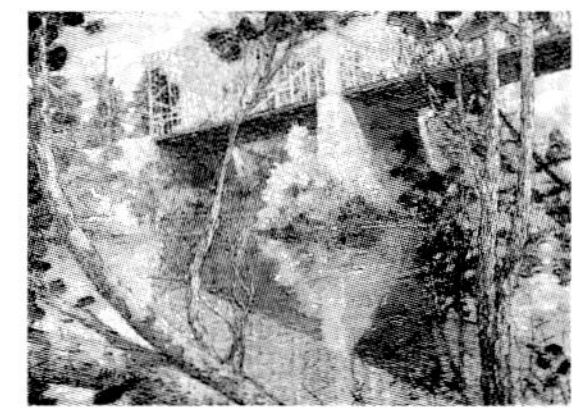

8. J. Alden Weir. *The Red Bridge.* 1895. Weir regretted the replacement of an old covered bridge over Connecticut's Shetucket River by a modern iron one. But he found in the new structure a stimulus for this composition, which suggests harmony between the natural and the constructed and provided him an opportunity to experiment with composition and color in emulation of Japanese prints.

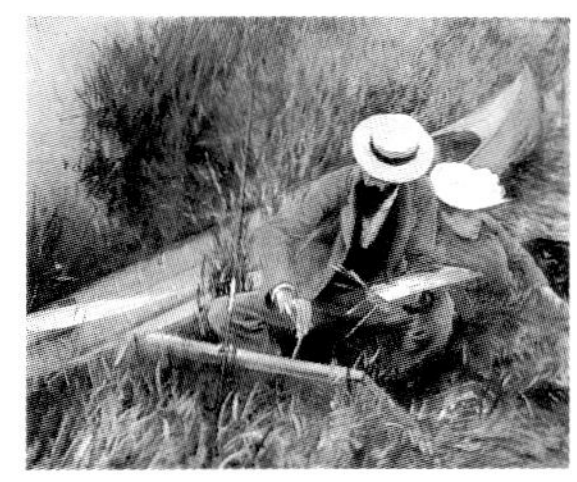

9. John Singer Sargent. *Paul Helleu Sketching with His Wife.* 1889. In 1889 Helleu—the French portraitist and Sargent's friend since his student days in Paris—and his young wife visited Fladbury Rectory in England, where the American was painting. Sargent's image of the couple suggests the importance of outdoor work—in the manner of Monet—for both himself and Helleu, who is shown here literally immersed in nature.

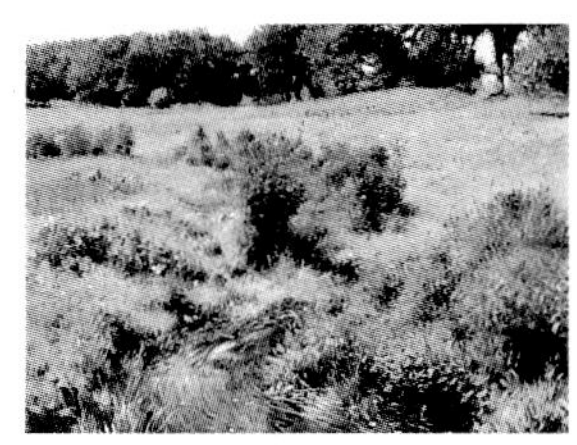

10. Dennis Miller Bunker. *The Pool, Medfield.* 1889. Having worked in England with Sargent in 1888, Bunker spent the following summer in Medfield, about fifteen miles southwest of Boston. His Medfield canvases reveal his mastery of Impressionist light, color, and rapid brushwork but are characterized by Bunker's hooklike strokes and interest in flat patterns.

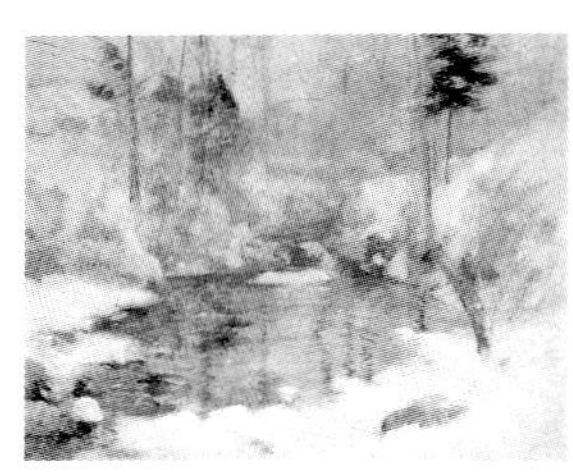

11. John Henry Twachtman. *Winter Harmony.* c.1890–1900. Twachtman made a specialty of Connecticut winter landscapes, especially views of the brooks and streams that peek out vividly from the confines of ice-covered banks. Like Weir, Bunker, and others, Twachtman Americanized Impressionism by his devotion to such New England sites.

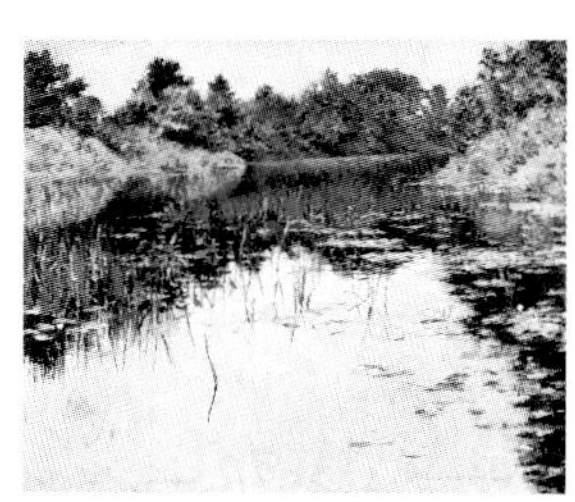

12. John Leslie Breck. *Grey Day on the Charles.* 1894. Breck's view is of an American analogue of the Seine or the Epte at Giverny, which Monet often painted. But his choice of the Charles River suggests that Breck was seeking a historically resonant place in which to create true counterparts of French Impressionist paintings.

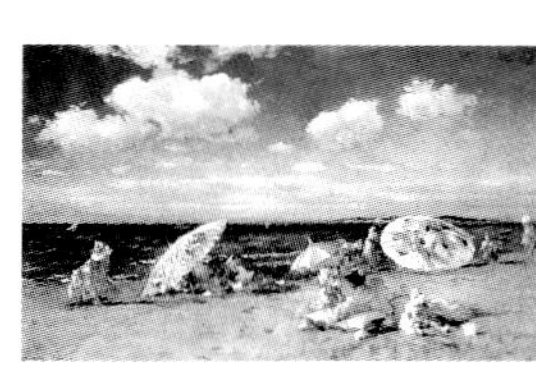

13. William Merritt Chase. *At the Seaside.* n.d. Shinnecock, where Chase painted and taught in the summers of the 1890s, is part of Southampton, an elegant summer resort. Chase's paintings, typified by brilliant light, vivacious stroke, and striking contrasts of complementary colors, reflect the increase in leisure time and the flourishing of country retreats for city dwellers.

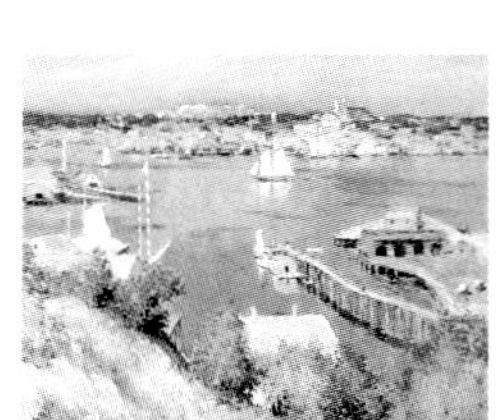

14. Willard Metcalf. *Gloucester Harbor.* 1895. Gloucester, like Southampton, was associated with colonial settlements and was also a popular venue for painters and a summer resort. It especially stimulated the American Impressionists, who enjoyed both its historical resonance and its extraordinary light.

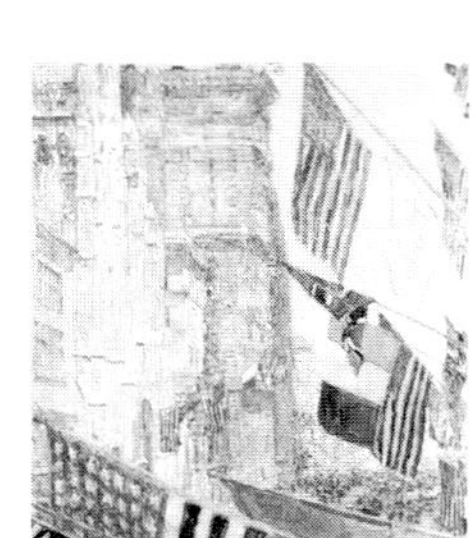

15. Frederick Childe Hassam. *Allies Day, May 1917.* 1917. An American counterpart of some of the flag-lined Parisian boulevards that Monet painted, Fifth Avenue draped in patriotic banners when the United States entered World War I was the perfect place for an American Impressionist's portrayal of a lively scene and his expression of national sentiment.

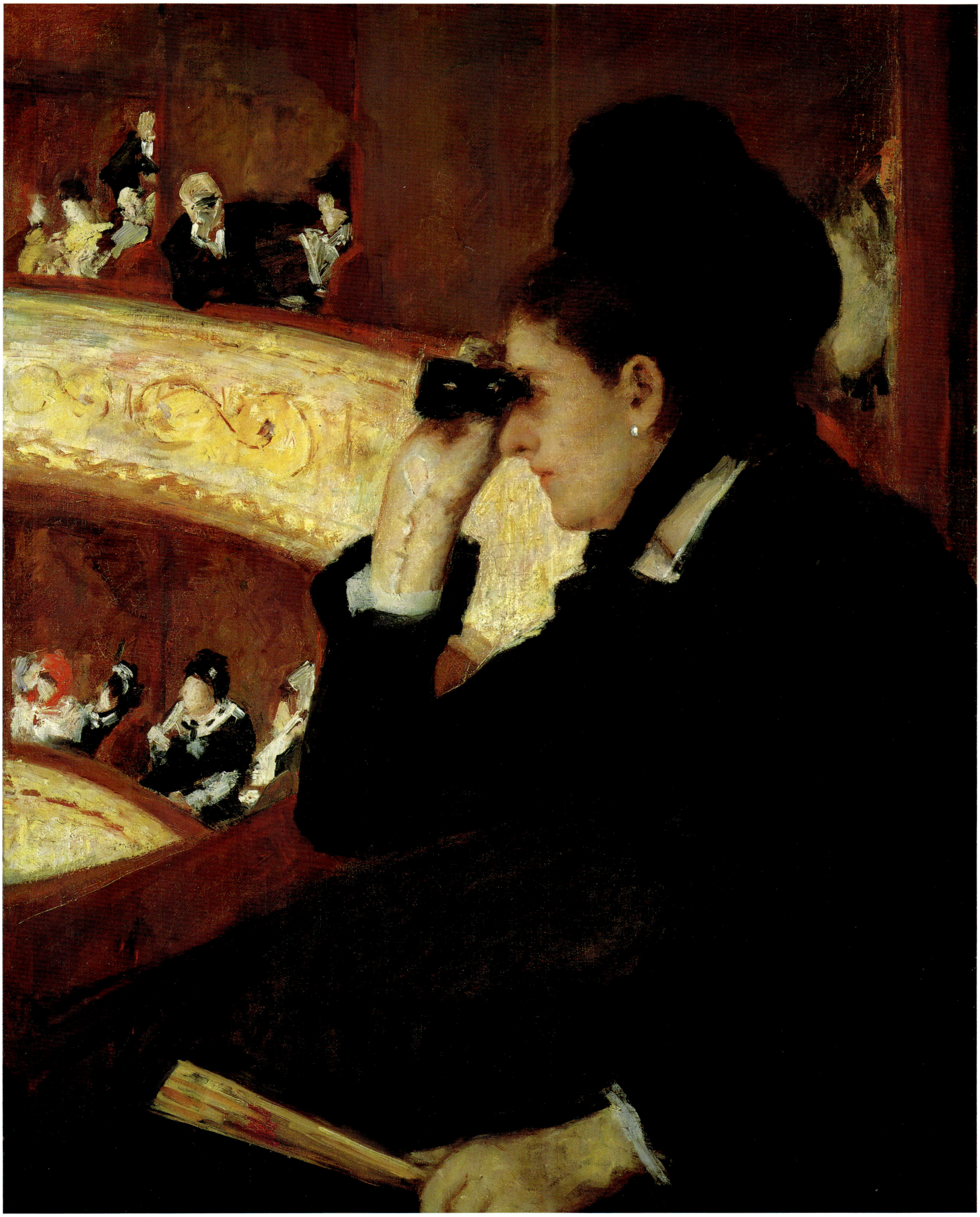

1. Mary Cassatt. *At the Opera.* 1879. Oil on canvas, 31½ × 25½". Courtesy Museum of Fine Arts, Boston. Charles Hayden Collection

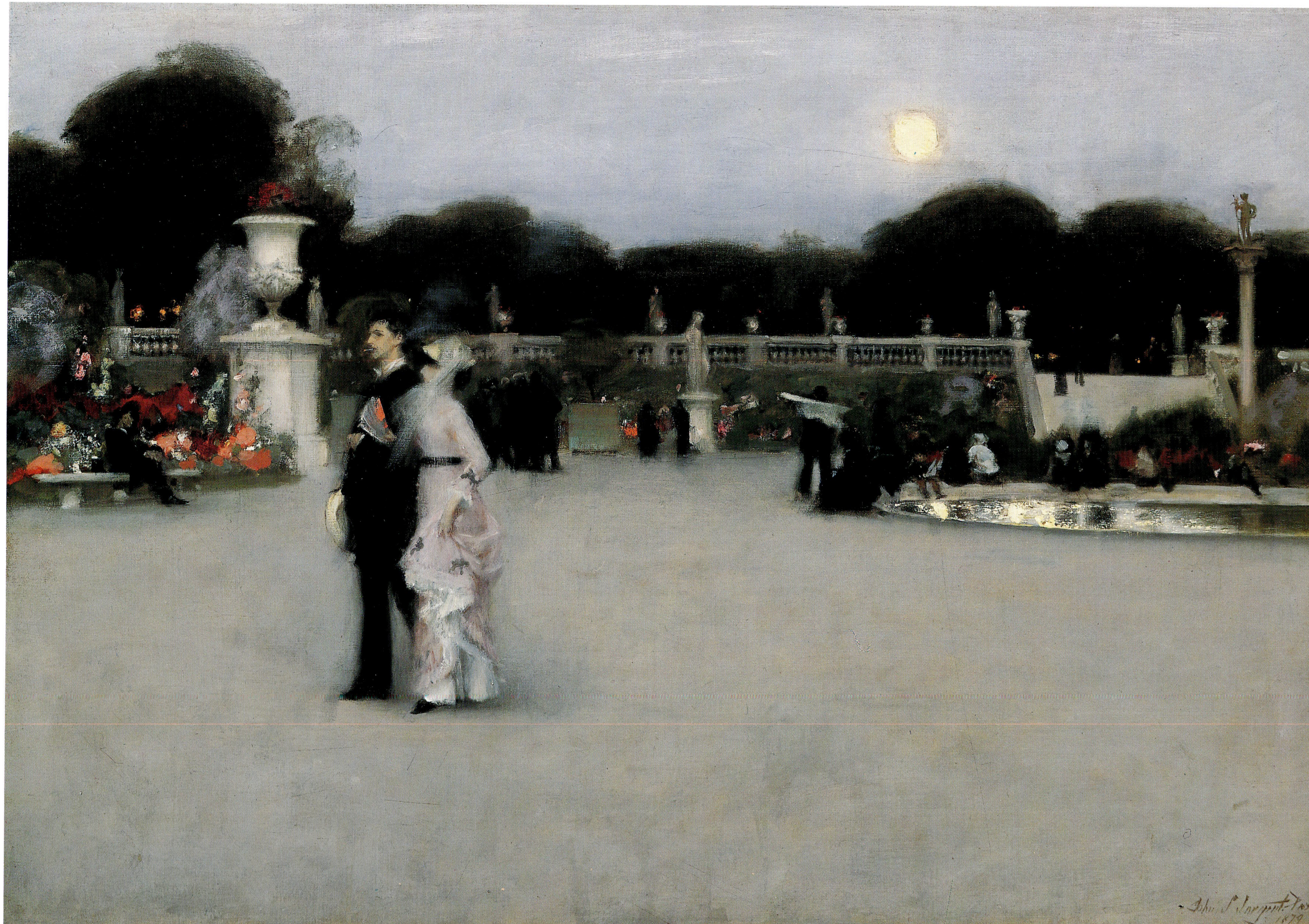

2. John Singer Sargent. *In the Luxembourg Gardens.* 1879. Oil on canvas, 25½ × 36".
Philadelphia Museum of Art, Philadelphia. John G. Johnson Collection

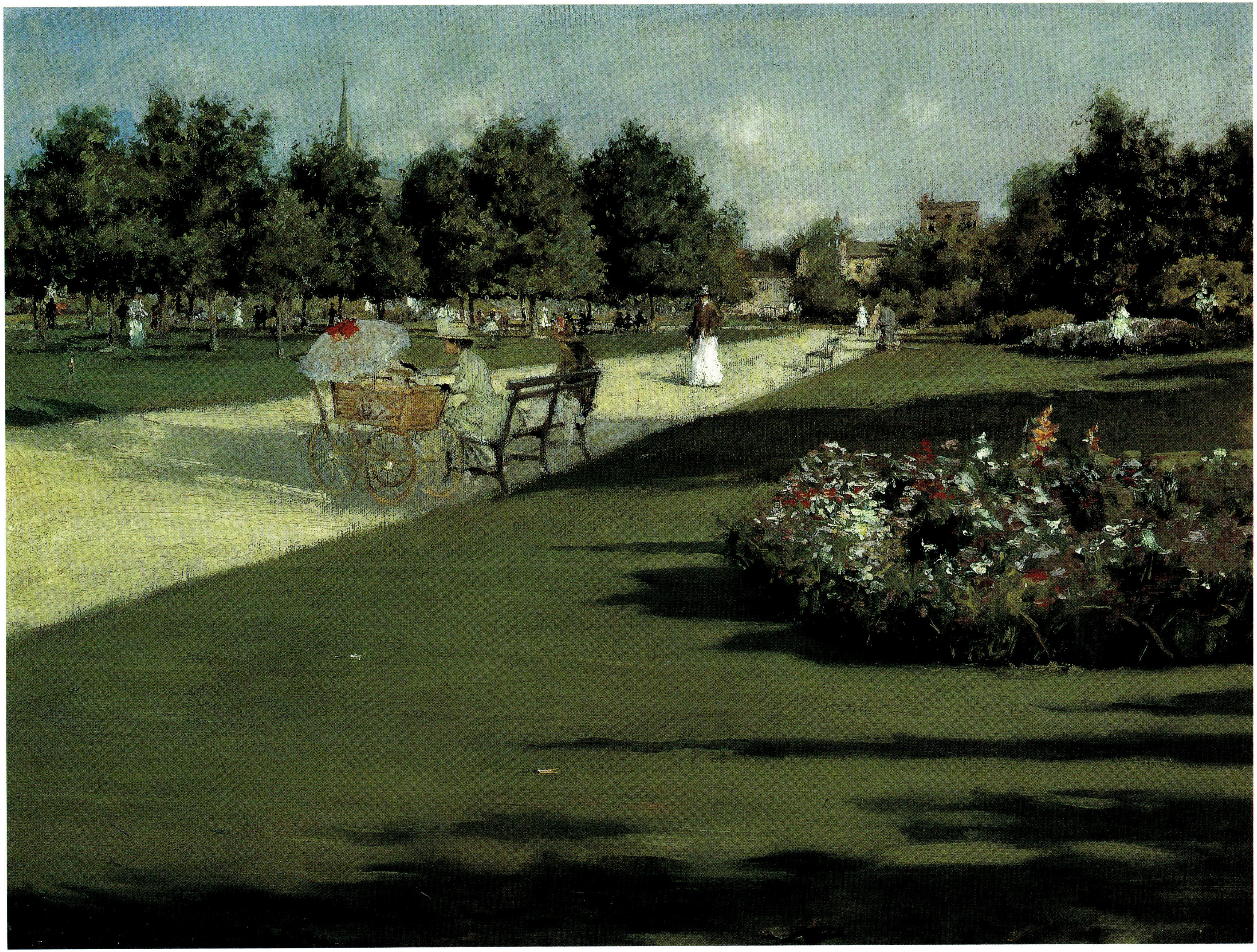

3. William Merritt Chase. *Prospect Park, Brooklyn.* c.1886. Oil on canvas, 17⅜ × 22⅜". Colby College Museum of Art, Waterville, Maine. Gift of Miss Adeline and Miss Caroline Wing

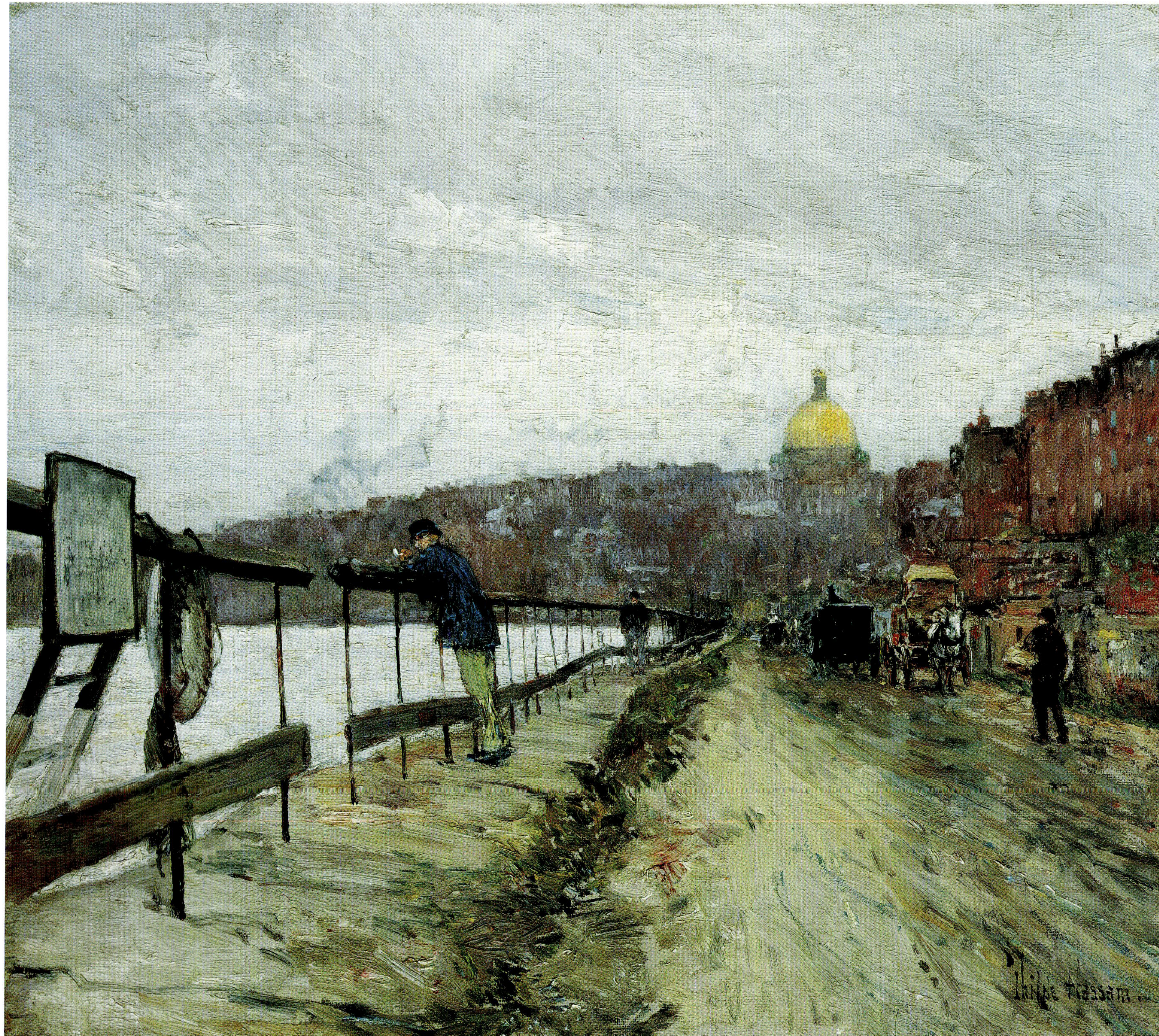

4. Frederick Childe Hassam. *Charles River and Beacon Hill.* c.1892. Oil on canvas, 18⅞ × 20⅞". Courtesy Museum of Fine Arts, Boston. Arthur Gordon Tompkins Collection

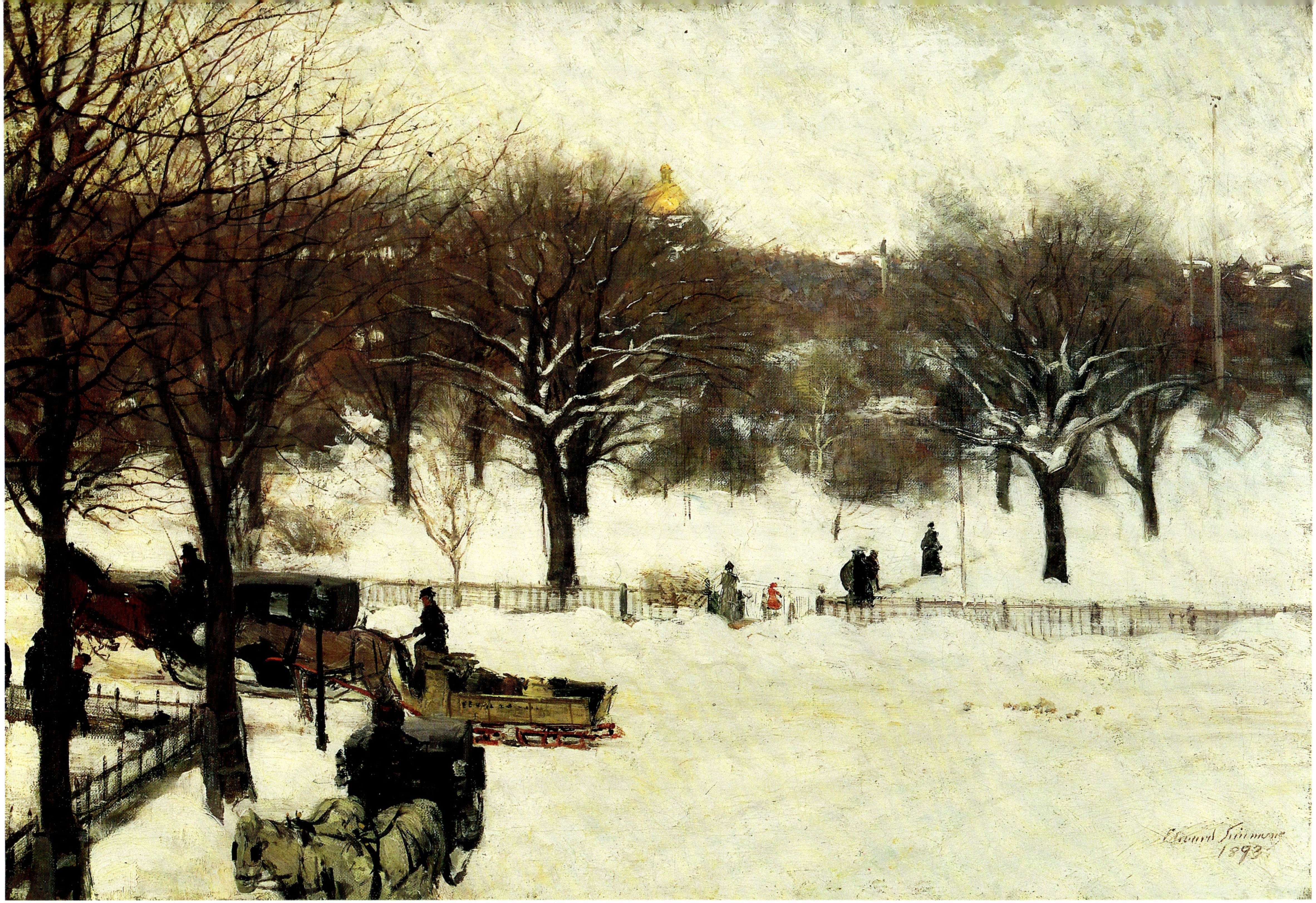

5. Edward Emerson Simmons. *Boston Public Garden.* 1893. Oil on canvas, 18 × 26". Courtesy Terra Museum of American Art, Chicago.
 Daniel J. Terra Collection, 34.1984

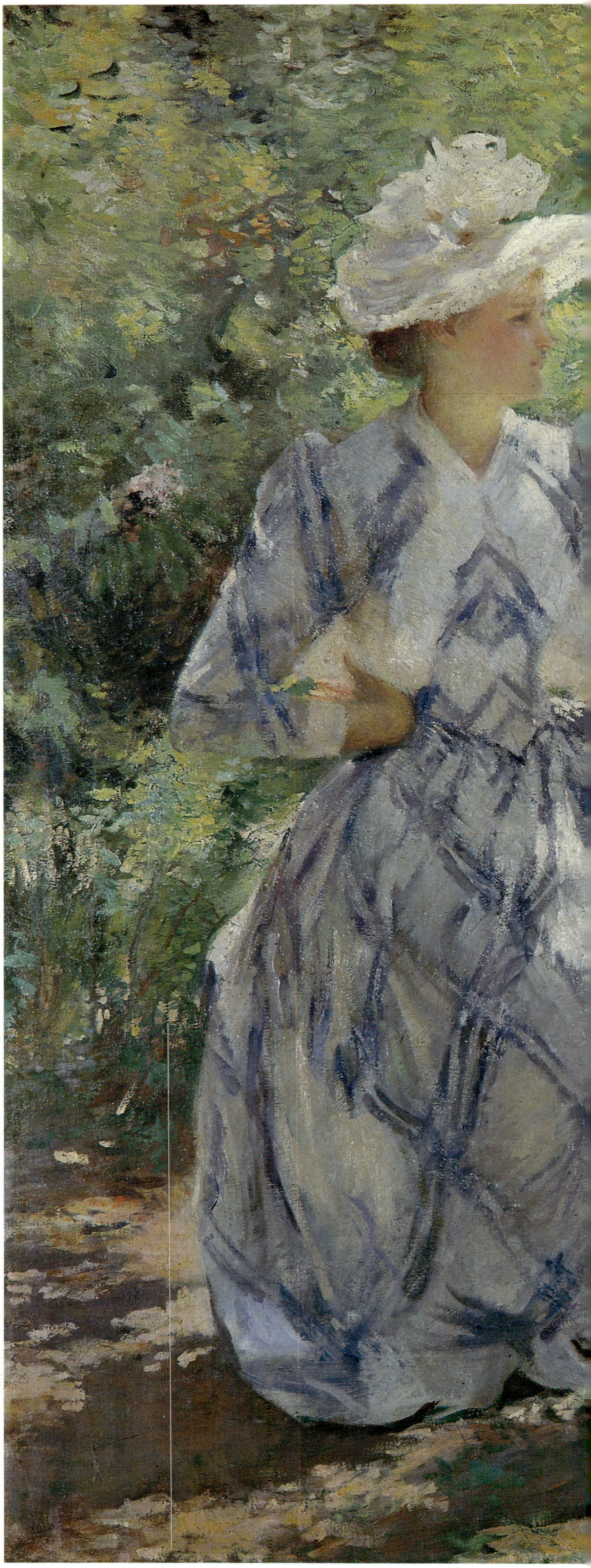

6. Edmund Tarbell. *Three Sisters: A Study in June Sunlight.* 1890. Oil on canvas, 35⅛ × 40⅛". Milwaukee Art Museum, Milwaukee. Gift of Mrs. Montgomery Sears

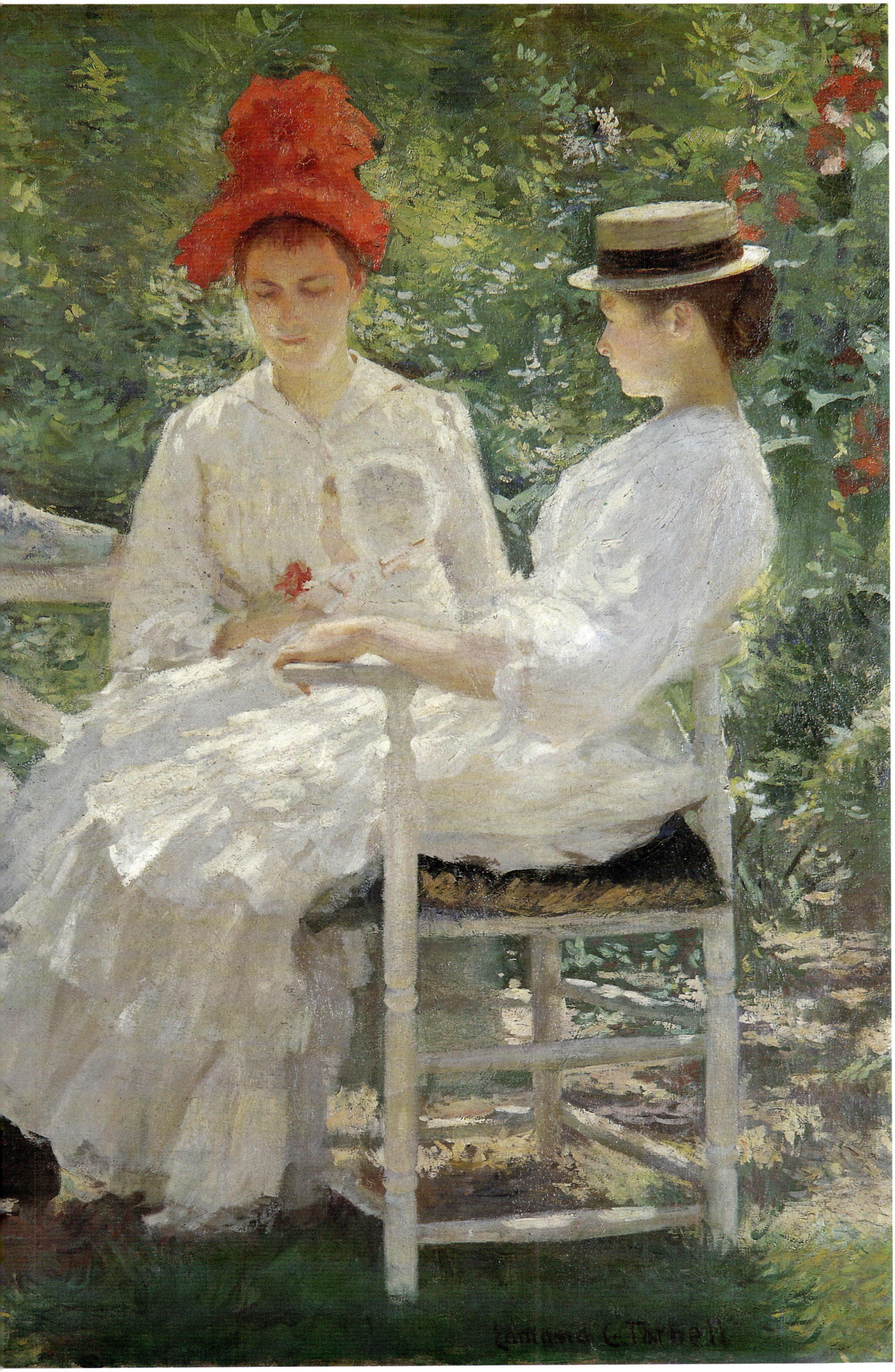

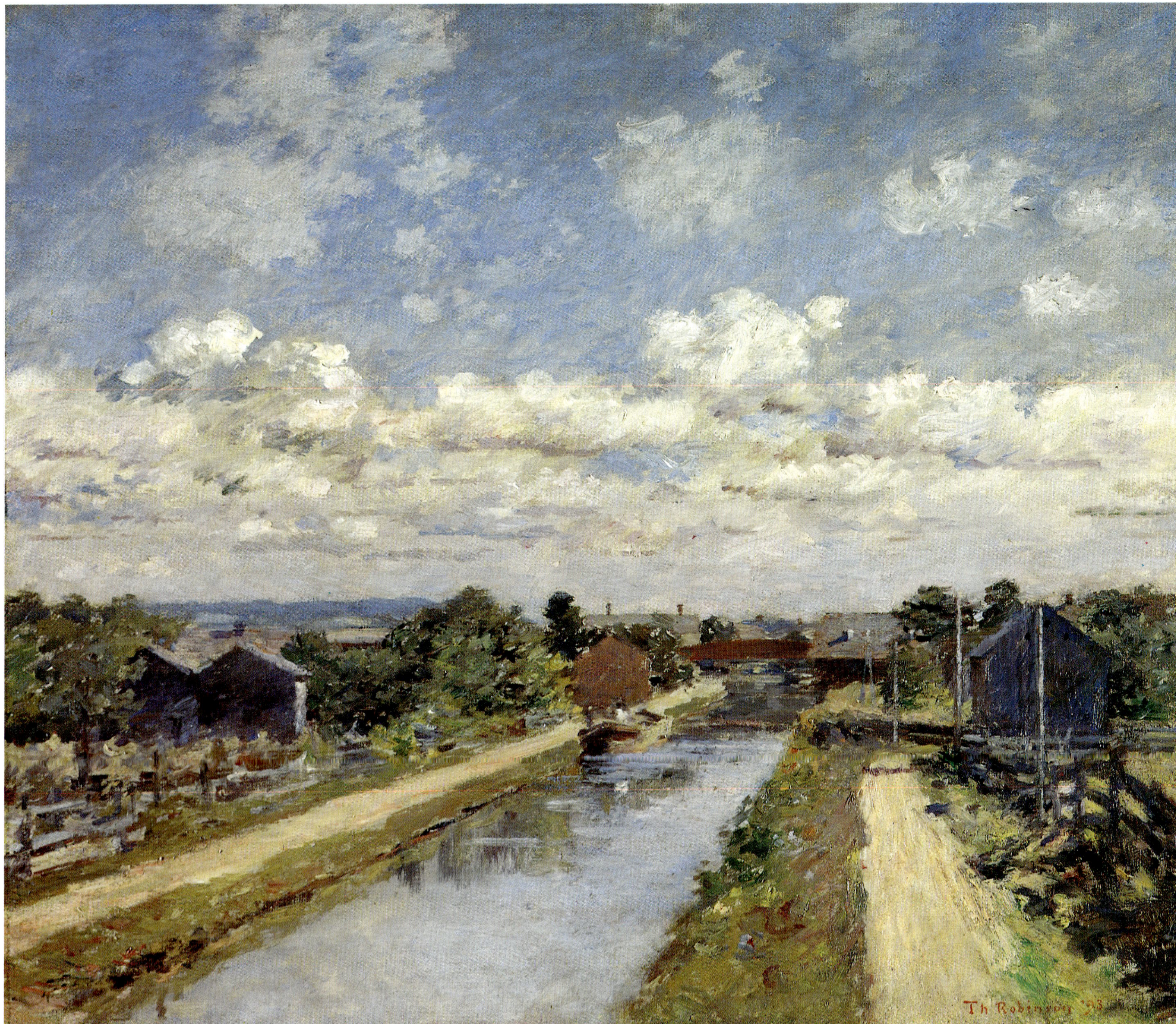

7. Theodore Robinson. *Port Ben, Delaware and Hudson Canal.* 1893. Oil on canvas, 28¼ × 32¼". Courtesy Pennsylvania Academy of the Fine Arts, Philadelphia.

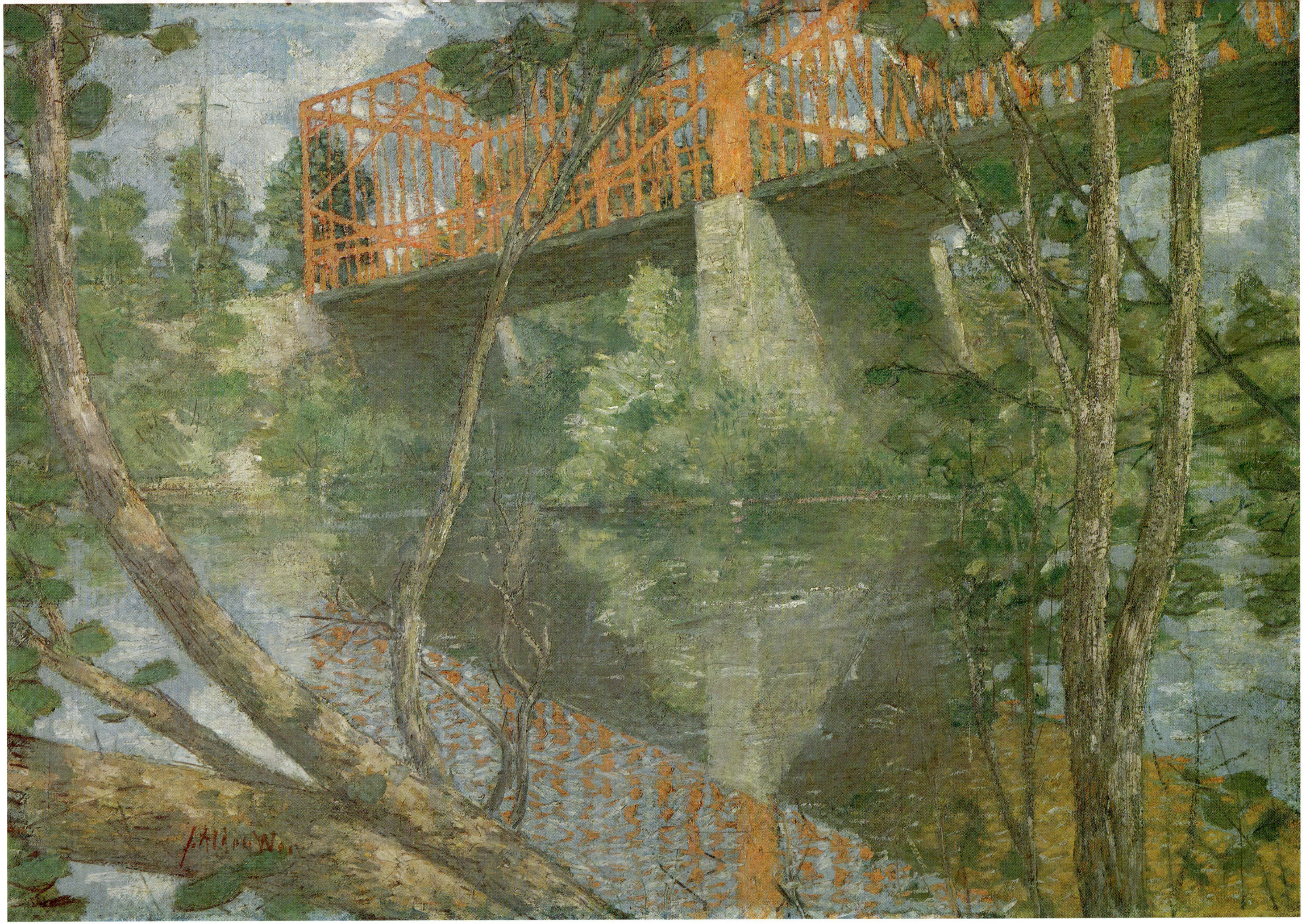

8. J. Alden Weir. *The Red Bridge*. 1895. Oil on canvas, 24¼ × 33¼". The Metropolitan Museum of Art, New York. Gift of Mrs. John A. Rutherford, 1914. (14.141)

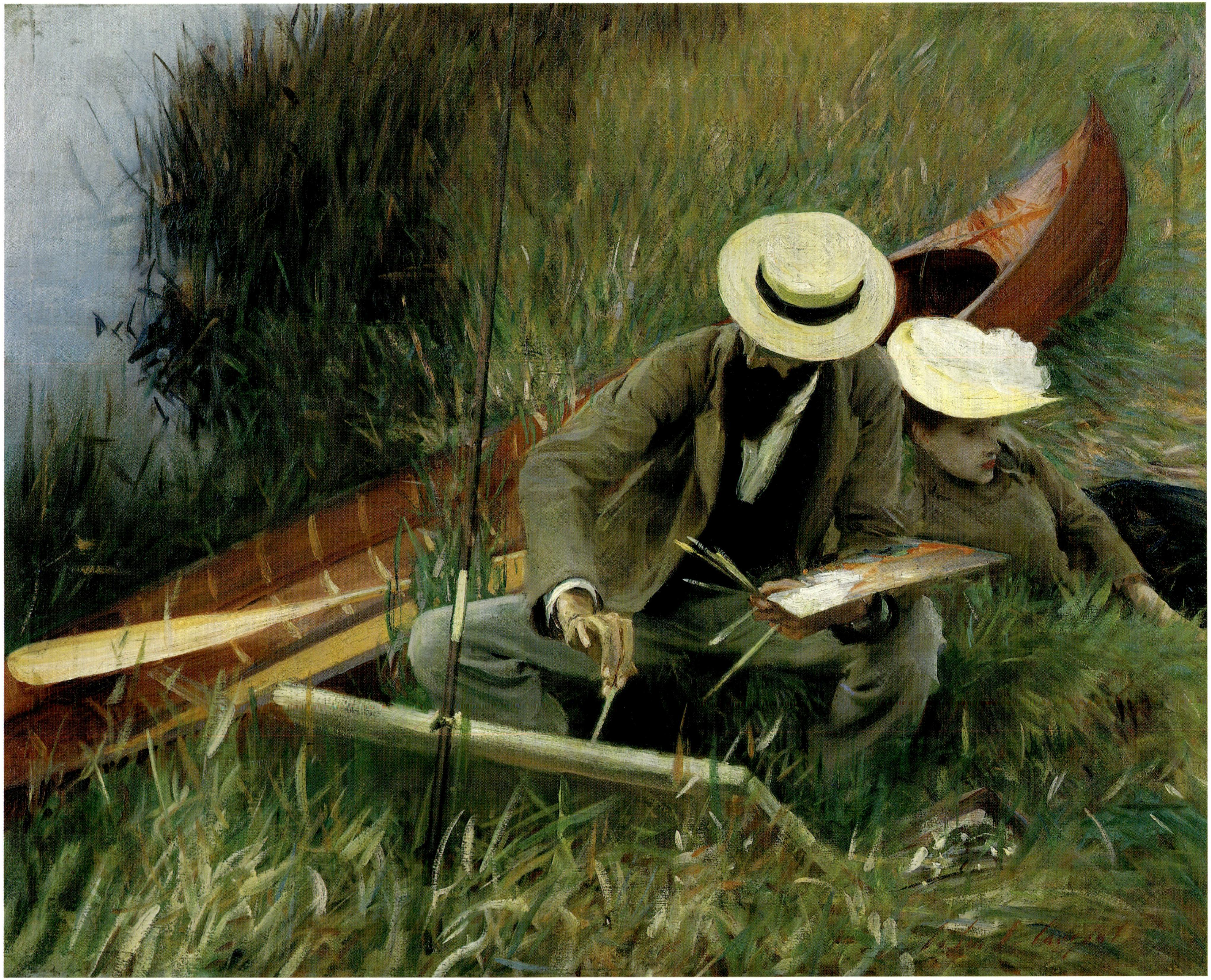

9. John Singer Sargent, *Paul Helleu Sketching with His Wife*, 1889. Oil on canvas, 26⅛ x 32⅛". The Brooklyn Museum, Museum Collection Fund

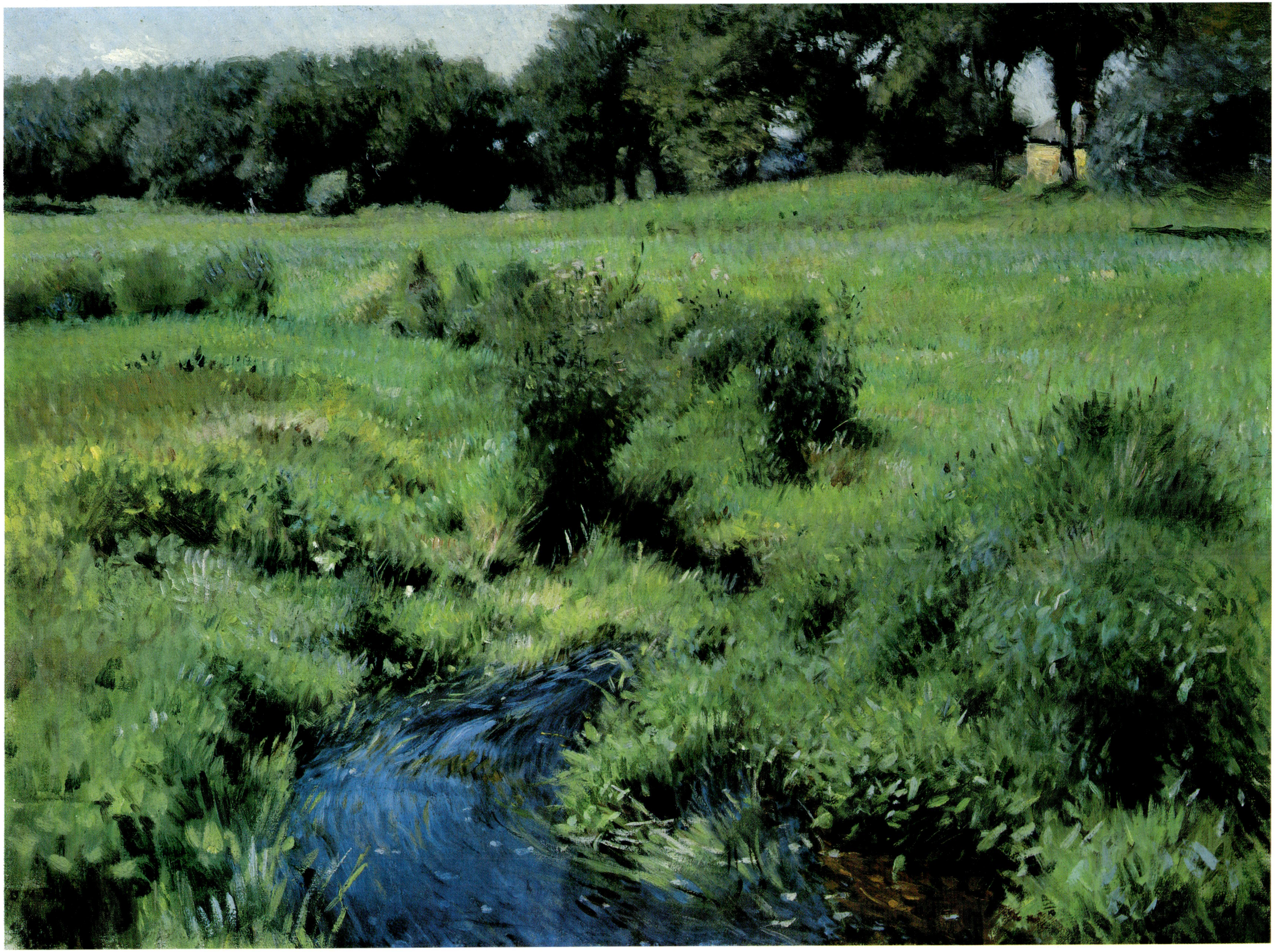

10. Dennis Miller Bunker. *The Pool, Medfield.* 1889. Oil on canvas, 18 × 24". Courtesy Museum of Fine Arts, Boston. Emily L. Ainsley Fund

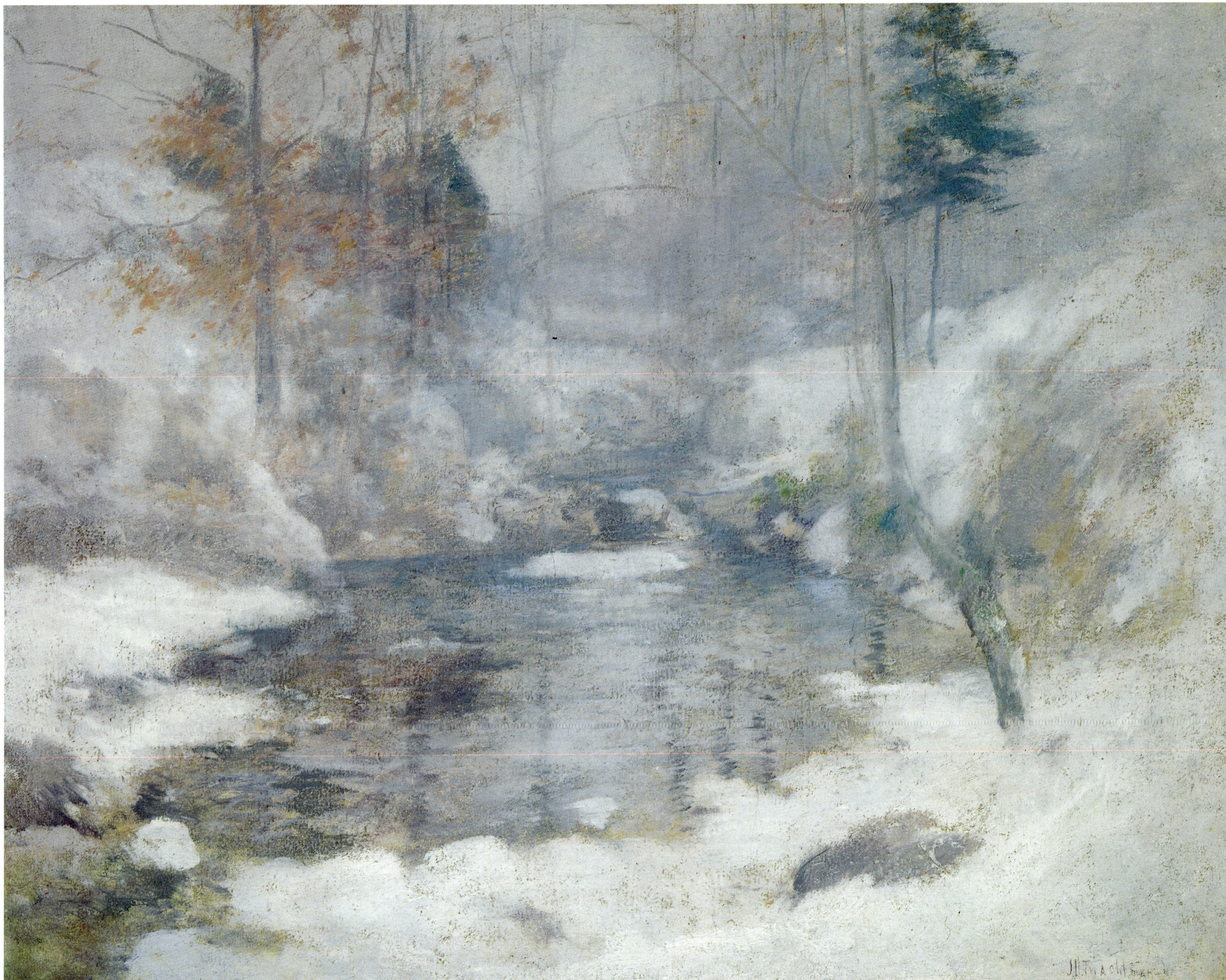

11. John Henry Twachtman. *Winter Harmony.* c.1890–1900. Oil on canvas, 25¾ × 32". © 1993 National Gallery of Art, Washington, D.C.

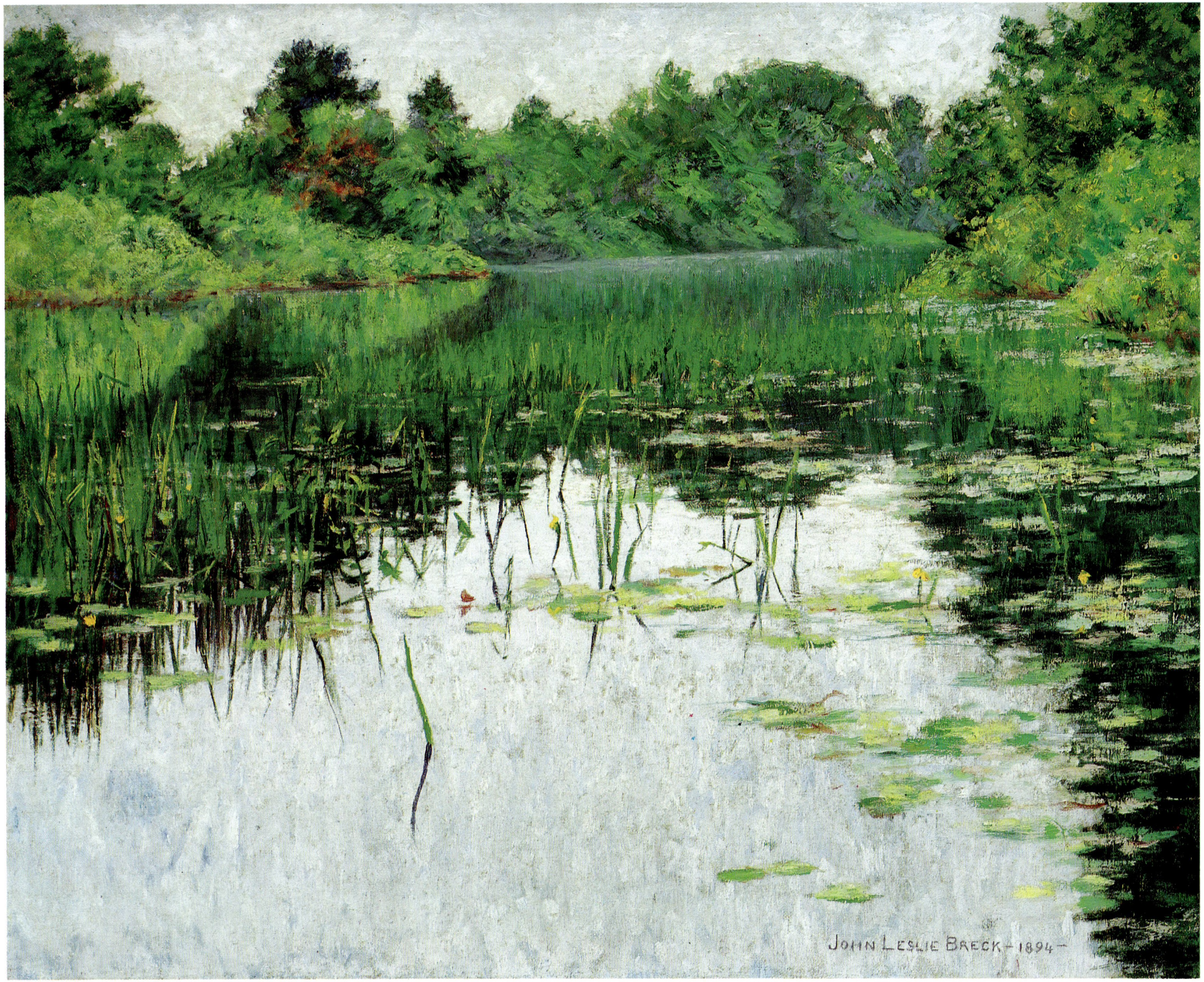

12. John Leslie Breck. *Grey Day on the Charles.* 1894. Oil on canvas, 18 × 22". Virginia Museum of Fine Arts, Richmond.
The J. Harwood and Louise B. Cochrane Fund for American Art

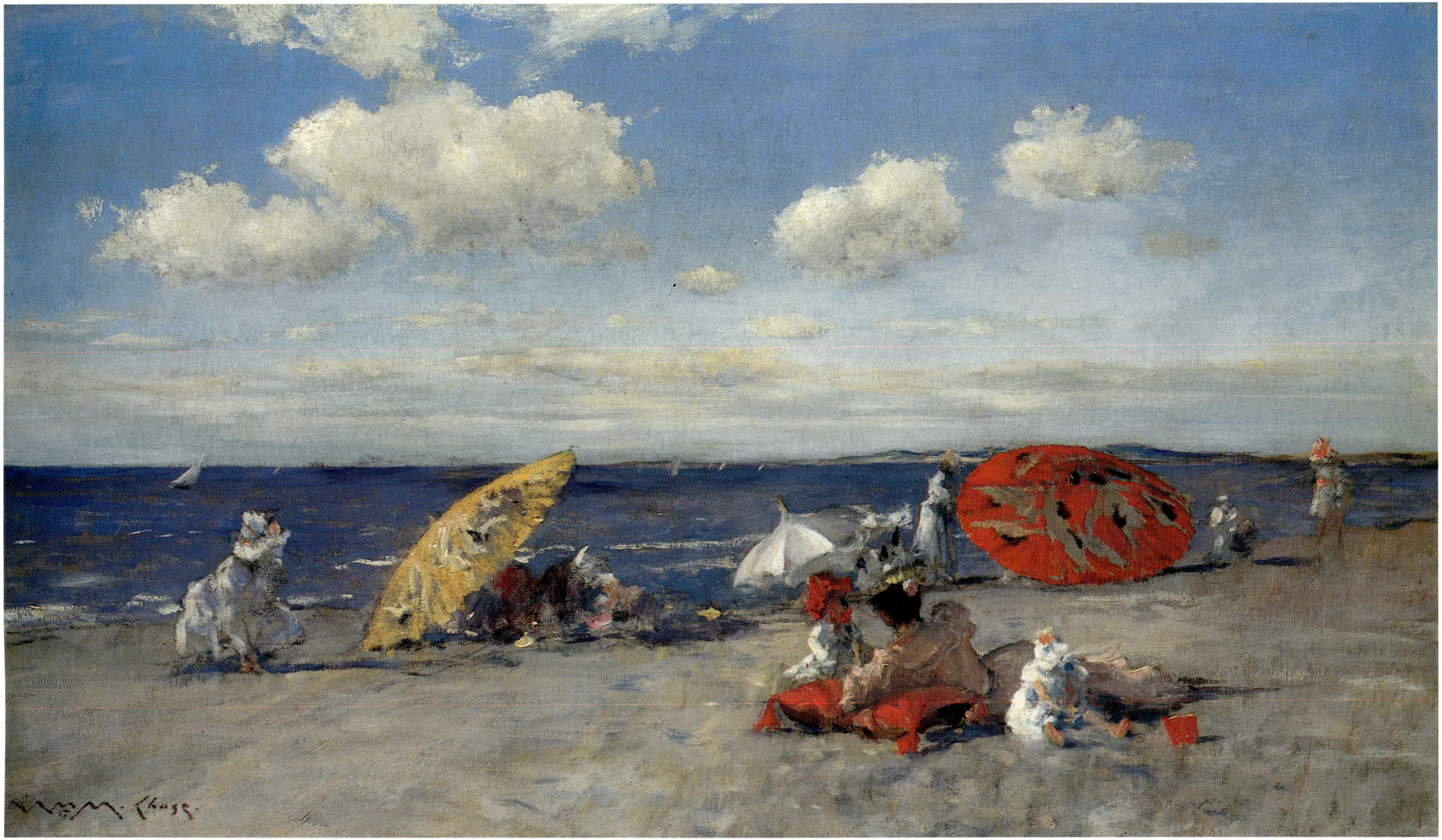

13. William Merritt Chase. *At the Seaside*. n.d. Oil on canvas, 20 × 34". The Metropolitan Museum of Art, New York. Bequest of Miss Adelaide Milton de Groot (1876–1967, 1967. 67.187.123)

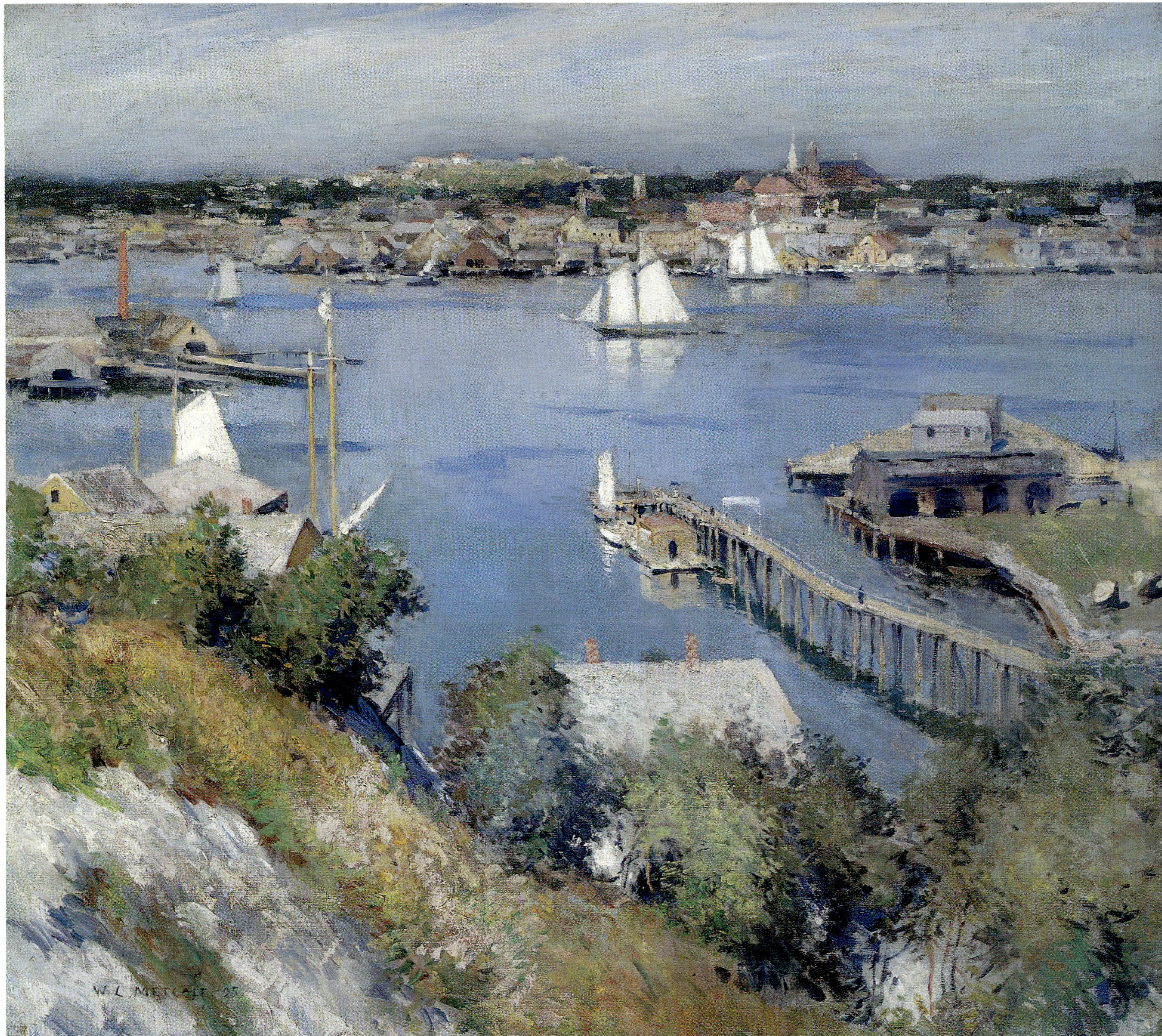

14. Willard Metcalf. *Gloucester Harbor.* 1895. Oil on canvas, 26 × 28¾". Mead Art Museum, Amherst College, Amherst, Massachusetts. Gift of George D. Pratt, class of 1893

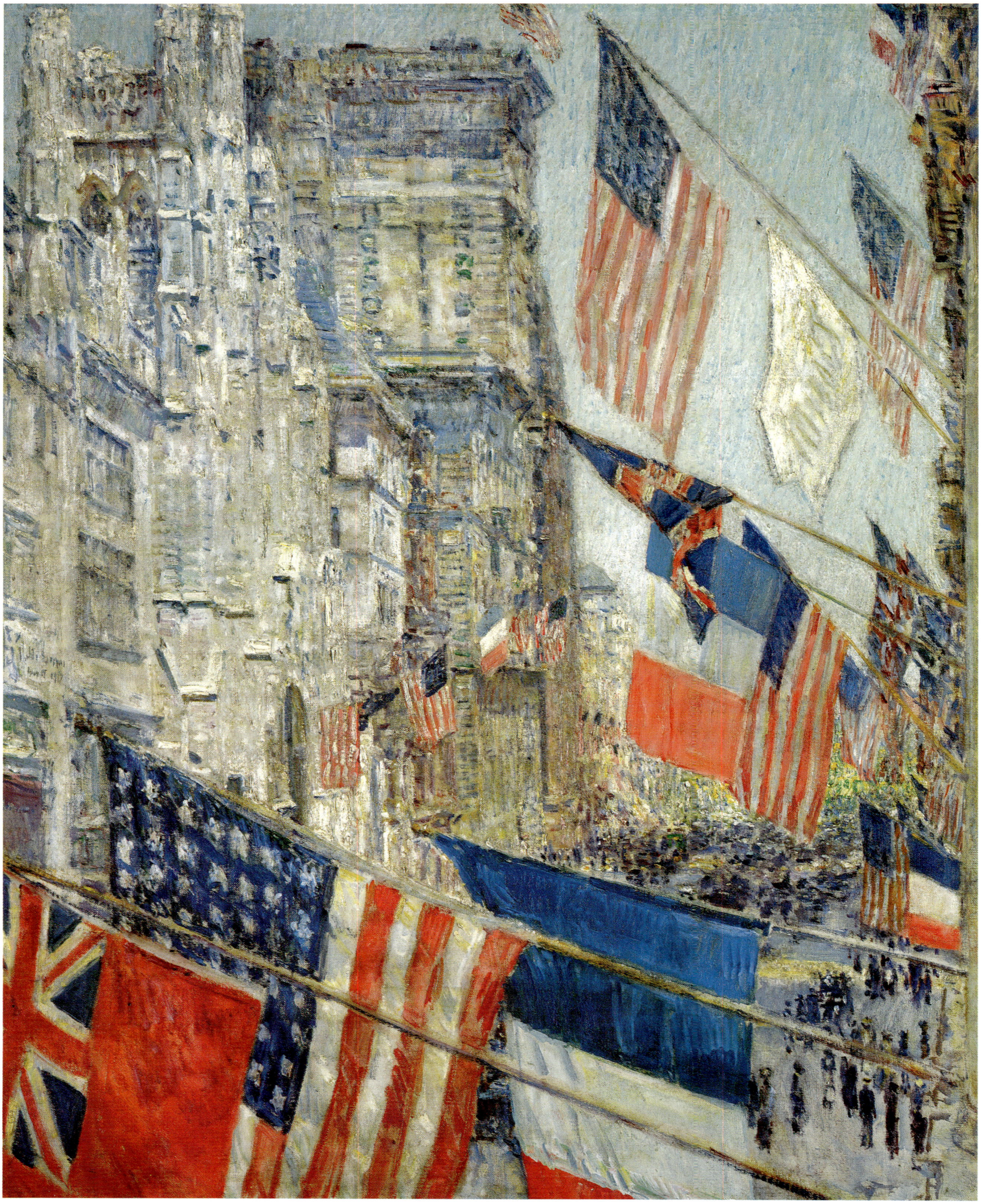

15. Frederick Childe Hassam. *Allies Day, May 1917.* 1917. Oil on canvas, 36½ × 30¼". © 1993 National Gallery of Art, Washington, D.C. Gift of Ethelyn McKinney in memory of her brother, Glenn Ford McKinney